Becky Evangelidis

Nothing to Hide

When control becomes out of control

Published in 2021 by The Tall Tales Publishing.

A CIP catalogue record for this book is available from the British Library.

Paperback ISBN: 978-1-9196491-0-8
eISBN: 978-1-9196491-1-5

www.thetalltales.com

Isaac, I will forever be indebted to you for saving my life. Thank you.

Foreword

A foreword is usually written by somebody other than the author, but I wanted to reach out to anybody who may read this book directly.

I wrote *Nothing to Hide* for many reasons. The main reason being I wanted to help other women. I feel the best way I can do this is by sharing my story. I feel one of the reasons why I found myself in a state of disbelief and not recognising the abusive relationship I was in was because I simply didn't know what abuse looked like in context. I also didn't fully understand the leverage of holding love for an abusive person and how that can translate into dangerous situations.

I don't know why you picked this book up, maybe you are here, maybe you've been here, maybe you're still healing or it all seems like a distant nightmare to you now. Take whatever you need from my story. Know that wherever you are, you're not alone.

Much love,
Becky
xxx

1.
Here I am

It felt so good to be in this moment. Sitting in the passenger seat, music blaring. A huge sense of 'I don't care' coursed through me. It had been a good few years since I had felt this free to be myself. I had spent a while trying to be the perfect girlfriend, and in the end we were too different. I had to let go of what I had with Ryan so we didn't spend any more years trying to make something fit that just, didn't. I had spent the past couple of weeks binge watching *Sex and the City*, barely eating, clearing out my wardrobe and redecorating my bedroom. I was ready to be over it. I was ready to be out there and be by myself again. So, I picked up the phone and called my best friend, Natalie.

"Hey!" I said to Natalie when she picked up.
"Hey Becks, how are you?" I could hear the concern in her soft voice.
"I'm good, actually. Ready to be getting back to me again," I said as I looked around my bedroom and took a breath. I felt good for the first time in a while.
"Oh I'm so happy you said that! Danielle and

I are going out tonight, are you coming?"
Natalie replied with so much excitement.
"YES! I'm in. I'm so ready to let my hair down and have a drink or two."
"Or ten!" Natalie replied. We both laughed, knowing that was exactly what was likely to happen. "I'll pick you up around 7, be ready!" Natalie instructed.
"Oh, I will be!" And with that, we hung up.

Gazing at the clothes I had kept, I started to pick everything out, trying to decide what to wear. Definitely not a dress, not in January. "It's far too cold" would be the excuse I would use to be able to cover my legs; I'd always been self-conscious about them. The colour of them was very patchy from steroid creams I had to use when I was younger. I'd suffered from psoriasis for pretty much the whole of my childhood and the creams had bleached parts of my skin. I settled on black, skinny jeans, a black and silver cami top that showed just enough cleavage and a silver, long-sleeved shrug because it was still winter after all. Not that I needed to wear them being just under 6ft tall, but the silver heels were a must. I loved wearing heels. I loved how they made my body look and made me feel so much more confident. I never wore heels whilst I was with Ryan, with him being an inch smaller than me barefoot, but this is not something I had to think about tonight. Tonight it was all about me. I was feeling good. I was looking good. I was ready to pick myself back up again and stop wallowing. I hadn't been out drinking and dancing for quite some time. Ryan didn't drink. We spent as much time together as we could outside of him working and studying and my university work. I wasn't left with much time to spend socialising the way I would have chosen to. I didn't mind not drinking – I definitely didn't miss spending time hungover. It was just good to let loose every once in a while; and it had definitely been a while.

As Natalie pulled through traffic and blared T-Pain from the speakers of her grey Proton Gen-2, I thought about the last time I saw her, about six months ago. She was married now and doing good for herself. She had always been ruthless in going after what she wanted. I loved that about her. I'd always wished I could be as ballsy as Natalie. Her car's leather interior was very smooth and comfortable, a good reflection of how she moved in her life. My best friend of eight years, we had been through thick and thin, for each other and with each other. She is the type of friend that everybody needs. Blunt, honest and warm, all at the same time. I was proud of her. Natalie had never lost sight of who she was – not like I had.

I started to think about how much I had neglected my own needs for the past two years. I pushed the button to lower my window, took a light out of my bag and put it to the L&B resting between my lips. As I lit and exhaled the smoke, I revelled in how much I had missed the taste of it. Not just the cigarette, but my own freedom. Ryan hadn't been controlling or tried to direct me in the way he wanted me to be. I had, of my own free will, neglected myself a lot. I had prioritised doing things *we* enjoyed over what *I* enjoyed, and in doing that I think I had lost a lot of myself. He was a good man. We had good times together. However, we were just two completely different people and, in reality, we came from two completely different worlds; we never would have worked long-term. I'd come to this realisation a while ago and it took me a few months to let go of him, but I knew that's what I needed to do. It was for the best for both of us. It just hurt like hell.

We pulled up outside Natalie's house and once we were inside, the drinks started flowing and going down nicely. I was going through a Malibu and lemonade phase. It was an easy drink that didn't give me too much of a hangover. The smell of the coconut reminded me of summer. I was definitely much happier in summer, when the weather was a lot warmer and the days were longer. I started to daydream about all the things I could do this summer without having to check plans with somebody else. It felt like a liberation. A friend I had at university had mentioned going to the USA to work at the summer camps. I remembered going to pick up the application forms together. They still sat on my desk at home. Maybe that would be my answer. There was so much of the world I wanted to see; it would be a good start. I was always nervous about travelling alone but maybe it was the kick I needed to build myself back up again. No boyfriends, no distractions, just me. I'd always had Niagara Falls, New York, Florida, Miami and Vegas on my bucket list. My absolute dream would have been to hire a Mustang and drive across the States. Now that I was flying solo, I couldn't think of anything better. So many sights to see and people to meet…

"Beck! Are you listening? Taxi is here, let's go!" Natalie snapped her fingers in my face to bring me back home to England.
"Oh shit, sorry," I mumbled as I gathered my thoughts, my bag and myself.
"Did you not hear him beeping? Where were you? You're not pining after Ryan are you?" Natalie said, giving me a raised eyebrow.
"No, I was just daydreaming, that's all." I'd always been a bit of a fantasist – a blessing and a curse.

As the three of us shuffled out of the door and into the taxi, we were so hyped up to be going out. I didn't know what the night had in store for me, but I was so happy to be in this moment with my best friend by my side. It was so long overdue.

2.
The first night

Last-minute plans are always the best. That night was the perfect reminder of where I needed to be. Natalie was like home to me. Being my friend for so long, she reminded me of everything I was, every way that I had grown and everything I had yet to be. Maybe I was too much in my own head that night, maybe it was the alcohol, maybe it was the change of scenery, but I was seeing everything I could be, by my own choice. I didn't have to grow *with* anybody; I could do it alone. I could shape myself to be the kind of woman *I* wanted me to be. Whatever it was that had me thinking this way, it was much needed. For the first time in a long time I felt alive.

I was happy for the night to be the three of us – myself, Natalie and Danielle. We were having such a good time dancing and drinking. When we moved on to the last club of the night, we bumped into Natalie's brother and a few of their friends that they grew up with. I already knew her brother but not the others. This would be the night that would change my entire life – the night that I met Aaron. It wasn't intentional. I was happy to focus on me for a while, but as fate or destiny or wherever it was had written it, this would be the night that my life altered its course in the most unexpected way.

We didn't talk much at first. It felt like the connection we had, just to dance together, was enough. It was alien to me. I had never been with somebody that was happy to go out dancing. Then, I met this stranger who didn't feel like much of a stranger. I knew that if I was in anyway unsafe, Natalie would have been the first person to tell me. She was such a protective friend, like the mother hen of our friendship circle, so I knew I was okay as long as she was around. There was something familiar about him. Something felt a little bit more like home than I had felt before. He was tall. I liked how tall he was. It made me feel protected and like I fitted in better. I wasn't the one who stood out. His eyes felt so familiar, like I could see a part of myself when I looked into them and he had the longest eyelashes. When we spoke, he had this reserve about him that drew me in. He was confident within himself and he didn't feel the need to be really loud or obnoxious.

He wasn't arrogant; he knew how to carry himself well – head high, shoulders back.

"So, how do you know Natalie?" he shouted, so I could hear over the music.
"We went to school together. We've been best friends since we were 13," I shouted back, hoping he got it.
"I've never seen you out with her. Do you not live close by?" He gestured with his hands as we sat in a booth close to the dance floor, close to the others.
"I live about ten minutes away from her mum and dad, so not too far." I could see a smile creeping up one side of his face as he looked at me. He stayed quiet for a moment, just staring into my face, as if he was taking it all in.
"Come on, it's waiting," he said as he stood up, grabbing my hand to help me to my feet. I pulled back and shrugged.
"What's waiting?" I asked, confused.
"The first night of the rest of our lives," he replied through a smile. I grinned back at him, stood up and followed his lead back to the dance floor.

This moment, this feeling, I didn't want it to end. How could somebody I had known a few hours make me feel as if I had never been without them? Was it the drink? Was it the atmosphere of the whole night? Was it the confidence I had in my new-found freedom? I couldn't put my finger on it. All I could think about was the words he had said to me. *"The first night of the rest of our lives"* kept echoing around my head. It was as if he could read my mind and he knew everything I had been through lately. That night gave me more than I ever could have anticipated, and it didn't end there.

The next morning, I woke up to Danielle asleep on the sofa opposite the one I was laying on. Natalie was in the kitchen making coffee. I sat up, placing my feet on the cold floor, stretched my arms out and took a moment for the memory of the night before to come back to me, and it had me smiling from ear to ear. I stood up and made my way into the kitchen where Natalie was. I was expecting an intense Q&A session, and that's exactly what I got.

"Soooo?" Natalie asked, grinning at me like the Cheshire Cat.
"So… what?" I replied trying to play down this huge bout of happy bubbling inside me.
"Don't give me that, Beck. What happened last night between you and Aaron?" she

asked, placing both hands on the counter and leaning towards me.
"Nothing. We danced, we talked…" I paused for a second, "That's it," I continued, much to Natalie's obvious disappointment.
"That's it? That's all I'm getting? Are you at least going to see him again? Tell me that." She was deflated by my response.
"I don't know. I hadn't planned on it. I didn't even get his number." I couldn't help but feel a pang of regret when the realisation hit, but he didn't ask and neither did I.
"Here," Natalie said, scrolling through her phone. "This is his Facebook. Just send him a message," Natalie suggested, trying to hold back her excitement as she flashed the screen on her phone my way.
"Wait, why am I sending *him* a message first?" I asked, trying to bring myself back down to earth.
"Because you can find him easily through me. He isn't so bold. He might not feel right in asking me for your name so he can find you." Natalie had a point. I rolled my eyes in defeat, took my phone out, found his profile and sent him a message. After all, I had nothing to lose.

After spending a few months of sending messages back and forth, meeting up, spending hours talking about music and travel, I felt like I had found somebody who 'got me'. I felt understood. I felt seen. There was a lot we had in common. He was so easy for me to open up to. I hadn't ever experienced what it was like to grow close to somebody that was so on my level. It was new and exciting. I was surprised at myself after having resolved to spend some time on me, and I hadn't had relationships or men in mind at all. Now, here I was, getting butterflies in my stomach at the sight of Aaron's name popping up on my phone screen when he sent me messages.

We started making plans together, starting with Majorca in the summer – a week away just the two of us. We talked about being exclusive. We spent a lot of time together. I started to make room for him in my life. I felt so comfortable with Aaron that I didn't think twice when he asked me to do small things. He would tell me he preferred a certain outfit or a particular hairstyle. The hints were so subtle. Like, he would see women in a magazine and comment on the hairstyles he liked and disliked or the clothes he thought looked nice. I really liked Aaron. I could see us going somewhere, and loved experimenting with my look anyway, so trying new hairstyles, makeup and outfits didn't phase me just because it was his suggestion.

The only disagreement Aaron and I had at this point was centred around how often we saw each other. I had never been one for confrontation, so when we had disagreements and Aaron would go quiet, it suited me. At least it did to begin with. In a short space of time, things got more intense. I came to realise that this quietness was the silent treatment. Aaron would block me out and shut down communication, so I had to start asking for things that should be freely given in a relationship. The feeling of being shut out from something that felt so familiar, so much like home, felt like rejection. I would feel the need to make things right and get back home just to avoid feeling so isolated. The silent treatment was only the beginning though. Things were about to escalate to a level I never thought possible. And the worst part was that I never saw it coming.

3.
Jealousy is the ugliest trait

It was 2:30am and I was outside, pacing the streets, with tears of hurt and anger rolling down my face, mascara staining my cheeks with black streams. I never wore waterproof, as I'd never been a fan of how long it takes to remove. It was barely spring yet and the cold of the night air stung my skin. As I wandered aimlessly around the streets, I was fighting the urge to just stop and lay down where I stood. My legs felt heavy and my body was aching. I needed sleep. Every time I caught sight of where I was, it wasn't long before tears blurred up my vision again and I was wiping them out of my view so I could at least stay a little vigilant. Who was I kidding?

My mind was so preoccupied with the argument we'd had that had pushed me out of Aaron's door, that I probably wouldn't have noticed if the ground had opened up and swallowed me into a new depth of hell. It felt as if I was halfway there already. How had our barely established relationship already reached the point of me having to storm out of Aaron's house to get away from arguing with him? I mean, we had met just three months ago, but it already felt like we had been through so much – like I had given up so much to try and make us work. Hearing Aaron say that maybe we shouldn't be together was like a punch to the stomach and it took the air right out of my lungs. It took me a good few seconds to remind myself to breathe in again. To hear him say that he was doubting us, that he was doubting me, all because I had a male friend seemed crazy. Especially as he had already told me that he loved me; I was taken by surprise at first, but I knew that I felt the same way he did. As I aimlessly roamed the streets like some sort of stray dog, the argument kept replaying in my mind. He had been going through my phone and had come across a text conversation between myself and James, a friend I'd had for years, from earlier that day.

"Why are you even texting him?" Aaron said as he thrust my phone back towards my face. It was pretty obvious he was angry.
"Because he's a friend, a good friend and has been for years." I took my phone back from him. James and I had met years earlier through mutual friends on social media. We had seen each other go through failed

relationships, new jobs, university applications, everything. We'd always been platonic. I had never once thought of James in a romantic capacity and I'm pretty sure he hadn't thought of me that way either.
"No man wants to be 'just friends' with a woman. They can never be 'just friends'. There's always one person that wants more." The look on Aaron's face said it all. He was so sure of what he was saying. I knew there was no reasoning with him. Not that I didn't try anyway. I still had a voice and I still had every right to defend myself.
"But we *are* just friends. He's never said he's interested in anything more and I know I'm not, otherwise I wouldn't be here with you, would I?" I wasn't trying to make him see that he was wrong about what he was saying. I wanted him to understand that the idea he had in his mind of how a friendship between a man and a woman is constructed is not applicable to me. I'd never cheated on anybody in my life; I wasn't about to start now. I'm trustworthy and loyal. That's what angered me most about what he was saying. It felt as if he didn't know me at all.
"All he is interested in is trying to bed you. Those messages are too flirty. That's not how I speak to my friends is it?" He said it so

matter-of-factly like he had already decided that I had cheated and that I didn't want to be with him. Quite frankly, I didn't know how Aaron spoke to his friends because I didn't go through his phone. He didn't even own a mobile of his own. After staring at me, waiting for my response, he turned his back and sat on the bed.

"I don't know what you want me to say. I'm not interested in James as anything more than a friend. I've not been flirting with him. I've never had any romantic interest in him at all. Why would I be here with you if I wanted to be with him?" I could feel the lump building up in my throat and my eyes beginning to sting. The feeling of panic was starting to set in. I walked over to where Aaron was and knelt on the floor beside him. I placed my hand over his. Could he really be serious about us breaking up over this?

"Don't lie to me. I've said I don't like you texting him, so you either stop texting him or we can't be together. It's that simple." The look in his eye told me he was deadly serious about this. An ultimatum seemed so extreme. It wasn't the first time I had found myself in this predicament with him.

"So, it's not enough for you that I cut Diane out, now I can't speak to James either?"

He glared at me and pushed my hand off his as he stood up and walked over to the window, keeping his back to me.
"I'm not arguing with you. I've told you what you've got to do for us to work and that's it!"

As I rose to my feet I wondered, how did I get this so wrong? Was I mistaken for wanting to keep my friendships *and* be in a relationship? Did that make me selfish? I grabbed my hoodie and flung it over my head. As I stretched my arms through the sleeves, I grabbed my scarf with one hand and bent down to pick my white Adidas trainers up with the other. I made my way to the front door. As I wrapped my scarf around my neck, I glanced back. He hadn't even flinched. He hadn't looked in my direction to see what I was doing. I half hoped he would stop me. As I stepped out of the house, I put my shoes on the doorstep and stepped into them as I walked away.

I wish I knew what I had said or done wrong so I could fix it. He kept asking what I was I was going to do. What was *my* choice going to be? I wasn't aware I had a choice. It didn't really feel like I did. I had to get out of his house and away from his interrogation. I felt so suffocated. Was it really supposed to be

THIS hard? I didn't deserve to be walking the streets at 2:30am because I had to get away from him and had nowhere to run to. I never anticipated a simple text conversation could cause such an issue. As I walked to the top of the street, my mind sunk back to Diane – it's not as if we hadn't been here before!

Diane was a girl that I became friends with after I met some of the people in Aaron's friendship group. He encouraged my friendship with her. I'd been out for drinks with her a few times and we would text to keep in touch. This same girl asked me for advice about her relationship and what she should do about her boyfriend, whom she had children with, cheating on her. I've always been a straight shooter and I don't give the spoonful of sugar with the medicine. I told her if she wasn't happy, then she should leave – especially considering he had done this sort of thing before. Did she find what I said acceptable? Nope. She hit back at me by saying I had no idea what I was talking about because I didn't have children and she wasn't about to take relationship advice from somebody who was in an on-off situation. Which was true – I didn't have children and I was in an on-off situation, with Aaron. If I had any sense (which I didn't) to walk away at any of the red flags I had seen up until this point, then I *really* should have walked away at this one. Threatening to "break my wrist if I carried on texting her" was not just a little red flag; it was a signal to jump out of the plane and hope my parachute worked! Yet I ignored it. Now, there I was walking the streets in the early hours because it seemed a much better option than to stay in his house arguing with him.

I didn't even know where it was I was walking to. I just knew that walking was the better option right now. I wanted to go home but it was far too unsafe to walk that way alone at that time of night. Who knows, maybe it would have been safer than setting foot back inside Aaron's house – that irony isn't lost on me!

I checked my phone – 3:30am! A whole hour of him not knowing where I was or if I was safe, and as I rolled my eyes, my phone started to vibrate in my hand. It's as if he knew I was looking at it. *You selfish bastard!* That's how I wanted to answer the phone but I was just too tired. I could have been lying dead in a ditch somewhere and it had taken a whole hour for him to call me to find out.

What could he have been doing for an entire 60 minutes that was more important than the immediate safety of the woman he claimed to care so much about? At this point I didn't care. I was just happy to get back to somewhere warm and relatively safe.

"Where have you been?" Aaron asked as I closed the door behind me. His tone was calm, like he knew exactly what I was about to say and how this whole situation was about to play out. He was always calm once he gained control.
"Out walking, thinking," I replied as I rubbed my hands together and lowered myself down to sit on the edge of his bed. I didn't bother to take my hoodie or scarf off – I still felt far too cold.
"And?" I could hear a tone of impatience rising in his voice. The look in his eye as he watched me was as if he was void of all emotion.
"And what?" I replied, knowing exactly what Aaron wanted to hear but I just couldn't bring myself to say it. I felt so angry – offended even – that he doubted my ability to stay faithful and not cheat.
"Well, have you decided what you're going to do?" He wanted me to say it out loud. It was

as if he knew full well that he was going to get his own way.
"James is just a friend. I'm with you because I want to be with you. I haven't tried to hide the fact I have male friends as well as female friends. I want us to be honest and open. I don't keep secrets from you." I spoke softly; the last thing I wanted was for this whole situation to escalate again. I looked him in the eyes from across the room. I was trying to read what Aaron was going to say next, but I couldn't.
"I only warn you about what men are like because I want to keep you safe. I'm scared of losing you. I don't want you to get used or taken advantage of, because you don't deserve it." Oh the irony! I took off my hoodie, trainers and scarf and lay down on his bed. He came across the room and lay down next to me, wrapping his arms around me. I tried to fall asleep, as I had an early lecture at uni in the morning but I was too cold and unable to relax. I was so confused as to why didn't he trust me. I couldn't understand what it was that I was supposed to have done wrong. I felt guilty because he was obviously upset and I had been the cause of that. As I lay there feeling deflated and restless,

eventually my eyes felt so heavy they closed
and I managed to drift off to sleep.

4.
Piece by piece – I was disappearing

I woke up at 8:30am the next morning and sprung out of bed. Fuck! I was late. Even if by some miracle I had managed to get to the bus stop 25 minutes ago, I'd never be at uni in time for my first lecture. After the panic wore off, the tiredness hit me like a bus of its own. I had a sinking feeling in my stomach. I was so frustrated with myself for allowing Aaron to suck me back in again. Only this time it had cost me a friendship. I just felt like I couldn't let go of Aaron, but I could never put my finger on why. I started to notice a sinking feeling, like déjà vu. I just couldn't figure out what it was.

Aaron was starting to establish a pattern of how he handled the situation each time we had a disagreement. I would be to blame for something that probably wouldn't have been an issue in a "healthy" relationship. He would make me feel incapable of making my own decisions, which would leave me feeling grateful for what he called his "help". He would knock me down to a point so low it made his own level look like the Holy Grail.

The 'Holy Grail' was always so out of reach. Sometimes I would get close, but never quite all the way there. This made sure I never had confidence in myself or my own abilities. What good would I have been to him if I could think for myself, feel for myself, draw my own conclusions and speak up for myself? He had to make sure I believed that I needed him. His pattern left me feeling empty. The relief of us making up had started to fade. The hope that we were building – or rebuilding – something together was starting to slip away. I never felt fulfilled that we had solved a problem between us. I felt empty and kind of sad that the relationship had cost me a small part of myself. Over time, the reality sunk in that the emptiness was caused by the parts of me he had chipped away at whenever I needed to fix whatever problem it was that we came across. It was never him leaving parts of himself behind; it was always me. The solution to the problem never held enough room for me in my completeness moving forward.

We had had a lot of arguments before over my relationships with other people. These arguments had slowly built up a pattern of how he would manage to isolate me and keep me away from friends. He created an illusion that, in some way, those friends weren't any good for me. That their presence in my life brought out the worst in me. He had cut them off one by one until the only real friend I had left was Natalie. I didn't have contact with her; she just left the door open, as if she knew I would need to escape one day. Prior to this 'incident', I had stopped going out with a friend from college because Aaron had stated that she was a bad influence and I wouldn't usually behave how I did when I was around her. The friendship that I built with Diane was brought to an abrupt end. And then there was Claire.

Claire was one of my best friends during my uni days. We were on the same degree course, and after lectures we would walk into Liverpool town centre and shop for hours, often stopping for some Chinese food on Bold Street, too. It became almost routine for us to the point that we never used to ask each other what our plans would be after uni, we just knew. We spent some weekends drinking with friends at her house. Our friendship came to a premature end not long after I got into my relationship with Aaron. It seemed Aaron had an issue with me making my own plans in my own time, too. Text message conversations would often leave me feeling like there was no space for me to do what *I* wanted to do.

I'm just finished up at uni, popping into town to do some shopping so I can be over later if you like?

Oh, well if that's what you'd prefer to do! Who are you with?

I'm with Claire. What do you mean 'if that's what I'd prefer?'

Nothing. You go have fun shopping with your friend. I'll just wait around for you to be ready to come and see me.

Sorry, did you want me to come over earlier?

It would have been nice to be thought of but if you're too busy, I'll just see you later on.

I was staring at my phone, confused as to what the hell had just happened. I felt that guilt again. If I had thought he was waiting around for me, I wouldn't have gone to town to go shopping. I was walking down to town as my pace slowed, and I started to question whether I had done the right thing. I knew he wasn't waiting around to spend time with me;

he had just jumped on the opportunity to make something out of nothing, so he could manipulate his way into breaking down yet another friendship of mine. Surely he could have spared me for a few hours? Was I asking for too much? Should I have checked with him first? I'd never been in a position before where I had to check with somebody else before I made plans for myself. In fact, before I met Aaron, I had planned on keeping it me, myself and I. The sense of freedom had really started appealing to me.

We saw each other most nights, so I didn't see how much time we spent together being an issue. Of all the questions that went through my mind I never expected him to say what he had said. I really wish I hadn't cut my shopping trip short for this! I arrived at Aaron's house and he was clearly agitated and yet seemed barely bothered by me being there. As I walked into his room and put my bag and textbooks on his bed, I looked at him, waiting for a response. He stared at me with a cold, hardened look in his eye. He took a deep breath, sighed it out and started.

"You're early! Thought you'd still be out with Claire." His tone was quite low and clear, like somebody with authority.

"I knew something was bothering you, so I'd rather come here and sort things out." I sounded confident to begin with. I believed that by abandoning the plans I had already made, to come and see Aaron, I was avoiding a bigger argument.
"You shouldn't have bothered." Aaron rolled his eyes away and carry on with what he was doing on the computer. I suddenly questioned myself on whether I had read his whole tone wrong during our earlier conversation on the phone.
"Why not?"
"Because it's not like you're actually bothered about me anyway."
"I don't get where this is coming from." I could feel myself getting upset by the notion that I wasn't bothered about him. Is that what he really thought? Had I not made it obvious enough?
"Well, it's not as if you treat me as a priority, is it?" he said, turning his body on the chair he was sat on to face me. I could see his eyes reading my entire face, trying to figure out whether his words were having the right effect on me. They were!
"I do! We spend most nights together." I started to give an explanation, rushing through my words in a slight panic as I took a

step towards him.
"You've got no need to be hanging round in Liverpool when you're not at uni. I guess you'd just rather spend time with Claire than be with me." I could see his face looking hurt. Aaron turned back towards the computer and started aimlessly running the cursor around the screen. I locked my eyes back to the side of his face.
"Why would you even think that?"
"Because you feel like you can just decide last minute to do what you want, don't even bother to check with me and then I have to fit around you and your friends!" His tone was getting slightly angry. I could hear the frustration in his voice. This wasn't normal. This wasn't how normal people react to their girlfriend spending a few hours shopping.
"Not at all. I would have come straight over from uni if we had made plans." I tried to offer some comfort, but he had already shut himself off.
"I'm sick of not getting treated like a priority by you, Beck. Just go home," he said as he waved his hand to dismiss me.
"But…"
"I said, get out!"

Why did I feel so guilty? What had I actually done wrong? This was insane! I didn't even know anymore. I had let his issue with my friendship with James slide because I could understand. I understood how being cheated on and lied to in the past could leave Aaron feeling insecure and wary of any friends I had of the opposite sex. But Claire was a woman. Looking back, it's quite clear that this was his way of saying, "*You check with me BEFORE you make plans.*" It was another aspect of my life he wanted to control. I couldn't decide for myself what I wanted to do, when I wanted to do it and with whom. I had to seek permission. I valued my independence; it is one of my characteristics that I thrived on. He was the complete opposite. So dependent on me that he had to make sure it appeared to be the other way around otherwise I might just have come to my senses.

Bit by bit, I did let him chip away at my independence. At times, it was because I thought he had a genuinely valid point – sometimes because I thought he was being honest when he said the things I did were hurting him, and sometimes it was just easier to give in than to fight with him.

I went home that day, after Aaron had dismissed me from his house like I was some sort of hired help. I tried to clear my mind so I could spend a few hours catching up on uni work that I had fallen behind on. It was no use. I couldn't concentrate or even form a coherent thought. This was becoming a regular occurrence, too. I struggled to concentrate. I'd find myself reading the same line in a textbook four or five times in a row and still it didn't make sense. The deadlines for assignments were creeping up and I hadn't done half the work I usually had by this point. I wrote it off as being overtired and resorted to relaxing for the rest of the day.

I started to avoid Claire at uni and ignored her texts. It just wasn't worth the argument with Aaron. Trying to maintain a friendship was starting to become an uphill battle. I'd cut friends off before, mainly to help him feel more secure and happy. I was starting to see a shift. I was no longer changing myself and my life to help him; I was now doing it to avoid the confrontation with him. I was slowly selling my soul to the Devil. Once he chose to take issue with something, he was like a dog with a bone, so it seemed like the easier option to appease him rather than argue with him. Claire was a really good friend and I'd made a huge mistake pushing her away. The part that hurt the most was that I had now become one of those friends that had hurt me through the years.

5.
Once bitten, twice shy

As we got to know each other, we shared a lot about ourselves, with some of these things being intimate and taking us right back to our childhoods. Aaron shared with me the things that led to him feeling insecure and like he had always failed. He felt he had never been treated as a priority. Things that were a plausible excuse for him behaving the way he did sometimes. I always found this to be the basis of the reason I told myself that he was a good person – a good person with bad experiences.

I shared how I was cheated on by Ryan, he had chosen to resume a relationship with his ex-girlfriend in the early days of our own relationship. I opened up about never really feeling like I fit in anywhere and how certain "friends" hadn't thought twice about tearing me down to make themselves feel better. When I felt the time was right, I felt ready to share the secret I had kept to myself for so long. Something that was not only hard for me to open up about – but, also, I hadn't come to terms with.

Aaron had noticed, and had been vocal on the matter, that I was quite reserved when it came to sex and the physical aspects of our relationship. I had kept it to myself for the first few months but he insisted I could trust him and I should open up so he could help if it was possible. I questioned if I could tell him. Could I actually open up about this and try to tell somebody what I had been through? I had tried before. I had tried to tell the girl that I used to call my best friend, her reaction was enough to silence me into not speaking of the experience again.

It was a sunny day, late spring/early summertime. It was starting to warm up but the breeze was still fresh. We were at my grandparents' house, which was like the hub of the whole of my family. The house was set in the middle of the housing estate that we lived on, yet, somehow, it always seemed as if it stood out from the rest of the terraced houses. Everybody in my family loved to be there, to go there and to spend time there. Mum would drop me off there every morning at around 7am, before she had to be at work. I'd walk the short distance to school – it was just at the other end of the close where the house stood. I remember many summers where my sister, my cousins and I would race around the streets on our bikes, with the house being the finish line. Whenever Mum would take me to visit, there would always be somebody else there. My nan and grandad always opened their home to anybody that wanted to be there. And with Mum often working 16-hour days, I really cannot remember a time when that house didn't feel like my second home.

The house is the exact house I fantasised about owning when I was a grown-up. Not so much the location, but definitely the house itself. It was spacious, outside and in. There was always such a buzz of love and togetherness whenever I visited. There were always people around and although it was a big house, it was never empty. In the summer, the front garden was alive with shrubs that bloomed along the outside of the fence. A rowan tree stood tall, its branches leaning towards the house and nearly touching the windows of the front bedroom. The orange berries dotted the path leading to the front door, tempting wasps out of their hibernation every spring. Being the house on the end of the terrace, there was a path that led to the back garden running around the exposed side of the house. The whole family spent many summers in that back garden – barbecues, birthday parties, sunbathing, raising every child that came into our family there. Being covered half in flags of concrete and half in lawn, there was space to play football and practise handstands and cartwheels. The inside was always just as full – full of laughter, love, people coming and going, sibling fights and fall-outs.

Nobody ever thought twice about us being alone together, because he was somebody that the family trusted. I remember the sun beaming through the window in the bedroom that was situated upstairs at the front of the house. I remember I was wearing dungaree shorts that I had to unclip at the chest and pull down. I was laying on the bedroom floor and staring at the football-themed walls as I could feel his whole weight on top of me. The carpet was well worn, barely offering any cushioning for my back that was fully pressed against it. He wasn't inside me; he was rubbing himself against me with his shorts and underwear around his ankles and was explaining over and over again that "*This is how people have sex.*" I was maybe seven or eight years old at this point. That is my earliest memory I have of the sexual abuse I experienced as a child.

It carried on. I have various memories of various points throughout my childhood up until I was around 11 years old. When I told my best friend at the time, at the age of 15, I told her because I had reached a point of understanding that what I had experienced was wrong. He took something from me that I could never get back. Having been told by him that if I was to tell anybody we would both be taken away from our families and be put into 'care', I didn't know what else to do, so I turned to her. This is one of the worst mistakes I have ever made. Her reaction was to tell pretty much everybody who was in the same social circle as the three of us (he wasn't much older than me). The whole experience forced me back into silence and I hadn't talked about it or attempted to tell anybody else since then. Until I got to this point with Aaron.

I didn't go into the finer details when I told Aaron, but he got the point. From this, he also started to see why I wasn't overly sexual with him. He understood it; he just didn't like it.

"Thanks for trusting me enough with this. It couldn't have been easy for you to tell me," he said as we walked along the canal path that ran past the rear of his house.
"It's not easy to think about. I just tend to try and shut it out," I replied and shrugged it off. I didn't want to make it obvious that I was upset. I'd always been uncomfortable with displaying sadness or anger.
"I wish I could get him in a room on his own," said Aaron, making his anger towards the whole situation obvious.
"It wouldn't solve anything. The damage is already done, isn't it." I raised my head slightly and kept my eyes fixated ahead of us.
"No, but it would make *me* feel better…" he paused, "and you should have been helped the first time you tried to tell someone." He tried to sound reassuring.
"It is what it is."
"One thing I don't understand…" I wanted to stop talking about this but it was clear he had questions.
"And what's that?" I asked.
"If you were that young when it started, but 11 the last time it happened, you were old enough to know what was going on. Did you not tell him to stop? Or tell him you didn't want it?" He stopped in his tracks waiting for

my response. I felt confused, not quite knowing what he was getting at.
"I told him so many times that I didn't want to. I tried all sorts to make sure I wasn't left alone with him or in a situation where it could happen. But I was scared. He'd spent years telling me it was a choice of both of ours. He told me it would be the last time every time, that he would leave me alone if he could do it one more time. He told me social services would take us both away from our families if anybody found out. He told me I couldn't say anything to anybody. I felt trapped. He made my skin crawl. Nothing about any of it felt like I had a choice." I could feel anger rising in me and I could hear myself getting defensive.
"I get that when it first starts as young as you were. But at 11 years old, Beck, you must have wanted it to happen otherwise it wouldn't have. That's all I'm trying to say." He carried on walking along the canal from our standstill and I was in such a state of disbelief I just couldn't find the words to reply to him, any words. It was like they had all abandoned me and I'd had my voice snatched again on the spot. And that's exactly what had happened. *I had my voice snatched, again.*

Maybe I was wrong. Maybe this wasn't something that I needed to tell people about. Maybe this is something that I just had to chalk up as a bad memory and carry on, or I was looking at the whole thing in the wrong context. Only, it wasn't a bad memory in my head. It was a bad experience that had left a print all over my body.

If Aaron could conclude that I was struggling physically, then why would he question it being what it was? He was already dissatisfied with the sexual side of our relationship – something I felt guilty about because I knew this was on me. Throughout my teen years, I was reserved. I didn't go out every weekend kissing different people. I was so shy and didn't develop a natural curiosity for sex as early as everybody else did. I lost my virginity at 19 years old – to Ryan. The thought of putting myself in situations where I couldn't say no terrified me. So I avoided having boyfriends or being left alone with boys altogether.

It was different now. I had come to terms with my sexuality and the fact that, as a woman, men would actively seek these types of interactions. I just hadn't done a whole lot of exploring with it, and, to be quite honest, I was happy to take things as slowly as possible. I was happy with having a boyfriend. Just one man I could trust and feel safe with. It was only with Aaron that the safety felt a little shaky. I had my voice. I could say no whenever the thought of sex became too overwhelming. It wasn't without its backlash but that was to be expected given he was a male in his early 20s, and sex is a key part of getting to know somebody when you meet somebody new. It was when the backlash started becoming a regular and drawn-out process of my *no* becoming a *yes* that it became a huge issue.

It became a real problem for us when we were seeing each other so often. If the sex was on my terms, it would have happened when I was able to hold space for it physically, mentally and emotionally. I was never able to prepare myself for that because we saw a lot of each other and the whole process just became so overwhelming. This, in combination with, Aaron's 'mechanical' approach to sex and his sex drive being so much higher than my own meant that there was a lot of overwhelm and sex not feeling *safe* for me.

We had fallen into a cycle of *no* becoming an argument, becoming a barrage of abuse and insults, to becoming a *yes*. I thought that after I opened up to Aaron about what I had been through, and helped him to understand my seemingly low sex drive, it would help us move things forward by working together. What it actually did was it helped Aaron learn very quickly that my *no* can be badgered and emotionally blackmailed into a *yes*. I told myself so many times that it was still okay because my yes was still *my* yes, wasn't it? Sure, I had said no maybe an hour before and he had made it *really* obvious that he was unhappy about this – to the point where I felt safer giving in than I did standing my ground. I was sacrificing my physical safety for the sake of my mental safety and being so, so reckless with my emotional safety in the process. This was to avoid mentally going back to that time where I felt I had no choice. I just didn't see that this is exactly what I was doing to myself again. The only thing that had changed was the person and the persuasion tactics.

6.
Cheat to get ahead.

My phone smashed against the wall as I tried to wrap my head around what the hell had just happened. I couldn't believe what I was hearing. How on earth had this happened to me? How the fuck could Aaron do this to me? As I sat in my bedroom, on my bed, the silence in the room was deafening. I didn't have to throw my phone very far for it to hit a wall but when it did, I didn't even care that it wasn't in one piece anymore. I could feel the lump in my throat building and the tears starting to burn my eyes as they welled up. The whole conversation just kept replaying in my mind, and each time I heard it, I still couldn't make any sense of it.

"What the fuck were you doing in her car in the first place?" I could feel a prickly heat all over my skin as I tried to digest what Aaron was saying.
"She knew I was upset about us." This. This is all he had to offer as he tried to explain himself. He didn't sound so upset about it either. "She thinks I'm right. She thinks you're not showing me that you love me

enough. You're not proving it to me."
"Who the fuck is she to be putting her two cents in where it has no place being?" I could feel myself losing control. This was new to me. I didn't get angry often but I felt as if I was losing my grip on myself. "And why the fuck were you talking to her about things that are private? They're supposed to be between us. Isn't that exactly what you told me when I'd been speaking to Claire about us?"
"I'm sorry I just didn't think you were interested anymore." I was angry. His response really couldn't have sounded any more scripted!
"Not interested? If I wasn't interested, I wouldn't be so fucking upset, would I?" And, genuinely, I was upset. Aside from that, I also felt so foolish. That's the part that had me throwing my phone away – the fact that I had given so much to him. I was so angry; not at him for all of the demands he had made and the choices that didn't really feel like choices, but at myself for giving to those demands and making those choices. And for what?

Being brutally honest, it felt like the biggest middle finger Aaron could have given me. Here I was jumping through hoops. Ridiculous, unnecessary, demeaning hoops for him, and he couldn't give a damn whether I did or not. It was all just like some big experiment to him, so he could see how far I was willing to go to make things work. He was testing my boundaries to see how far he could manage to push me. He didn't respect my boundaries or take them seriously; he treated them as a challenge – like something I had put in place for him to conquer. No, they were there for a reason. I was constantly trying to make him happy. I knew he had been hurt. I've no idea why I felt the need to put the onus on myself to make that right when it wasn't my wrongdoing. I tried so hard to make him happy. Nothing I ever did was good enough for him. And now this. According to him and *Sarah*, I still wasn't doing enough. I still wasn't trying hard enough. I still wasn't giving enough. What the fuck did Sarah know anyway? Who even was she and where had she come from? I'd never met this woman and all of a sudden she was some sort of expert on our relationship.

So everything I had done thus far – which is DEFINITELY a lot more than most women would have done – wasn't enough for him. What the fuck would he deem as enough? I'd already destroyed my own boundaries to cater to his comfort. I was giving all I had to him and then some. Why the fuck did I have to *prove* how much I felt for him? Why did I need to *prove* anything? What was this proof doing for him that my time, effort and energy wasn't? It was like he was asking for something tangible from something that he had to feel. Everything he was asking for were things that would happen over time, but he wanted to see it, hear it, feel it, have it right there and then. I was just one woman – what the hell was he expecting? He was so insecure in himself that he was looking to me to fill those voids. I couldn't fill those voids and I had no business trying. But I tried anyway. That was my mistake.

I wiped my tears away, staining my sleeve black with mascara – with the amount of crying I'd done those past few months you'd think I'd have invested in a waterproof by now – and I took a deep breath. I had no idea how long I had just sat on the edge of my bed and cried for. I felt done. How could I let somebody I had known for five months make me feel so low? I knew that it would be best for me to just cut ties now and walk away; I was surely worth more than this? So that's what I made my mind up to do, right there and then. I picked my phone up off the floor, with my hands shaking, put it back together and turned it on. Within seconds, it was ringing…

"She's just a friend. *She* made a move on *me*. I don't even like her in that way." I felt another blow to the gut when he basically had just spelt out that he had cheated on me with a girl he didn't even like!
"You obviously weren't saying no though, were you!" I put my back to my door and slid down until I was sat on my floor. Bringing my knees to my chest, I wrapped my arm around them. I had numbed to everything. No emotions could be read from my voice. I just wanted to tell him that it was over and get the hell off the phone.
"I froze. I didn't know what to do. I felt like you didn't want to be with me." He paused, took a deep breath to slow his words down, then continued, "You weren't showing me enough. Then she's there showing me everything I wanted."
"Oh I'll bet she was! How the fuck can you say to me I don't want to be with you. That I'm not showing you enough. I don't know what more I can do." Everything, EVERYTHING I had done thus far ran

through my mind. Skipping classes, cutting friends loose, changing my behaviour, my makeup, my hair, my clothes – all for nothing, so it seemed.
"Well, it's something we'll have to work on, won't we." He fired that at me like word vomit he had no chance of stopping.
"I'm sorry, *we*?" I lowered my tone in shock. It suddenly dawned on me that he thought this wasn't going to break us up; he was saying this was just a bump in the road.
"You can't let this get in the way. I honestly thought you were ready to call it a day. You were doing nothing at all to make us work."
Nothing. At. All?
"I tried. I tried my fucking best. But not after this!" I shouted, knowing I was over this. Even if he was right in what he thought was me not being interested anymore, he didn't even have the courtesy to wait until we had called it quits!

I wasn't going to argue with him. If he couldn't see and appreciate that I was doing everything he asked of me, no matter how unreasonable it was, then I wasn't going to make him see it. I hung up the phone and put it on silent. I walked to my desk to set my phone down and it took no time at all for him to leave a voicemail, the notification flashing across the screen before the phone had even left my hand. And just like that, he was angry sobbing. I mean, he was really raging down the phone.

"You have one new message," the automated voice beeped in…
"Beck, I honestly can't believe you'd walk away over something like this. This wasn't my fault. I didn't see it coming until she was all over me. I just wanted you to love me. I needed you. I still need you. Pick the phone up. Pick the fucking phone up or I'll come over. I'll be banging on your front door soon. You promised you'd be there for me no matter what. I fucking hate you. If I ever see you again, you'll be sorry. You don't get to fuck me over like this. I need you. I'm going to go for a walk. Don't be surprised if you don't hear from me again. I can't take this anymore. And this is on you." The message ended.

Just like that he had reeled me back in. Like a fool who didn't know any better, I bit down on it and I got hooked. I panicked. I will admit I panicked. I was terrified of the state he had got himself into. I'd never heard him like that before. The sheer anger in his voice was so intimidating, yet I knew it was coming from a place of pain. I knew I couldn't handle it if he did something neither of us could take back. He knew this, too. He could see I was the sensitive type. He saw it in me before I saw it in myself. Of course, he had absolutely no problem with exploiting this for his own benefit. Telling me how broken *he* was, what *he* needed to be fixed and how he thought I could be the one to do that for him. This was his opportunity to give his insane standards a bit of clout, wasn't it? He created a situation that would display how messed up and vulnerable he was and then he used it to ask me to be the one to fix it all for him, to be the answer to his prayers and make all of his pain melt away. He painted a vivid picture of something I may finally be able to do right for him, because before now, I'd gotten most things wrong.

I had to be under the impression that he was wanted by other women. He had to make it crystal clear he had other options. How else could he make sure I would be quick to step up to the plate? He had this "friend" who was like a best friend to him that he, funnily enough, had never mentioned up until now. This friend was there for him, to console him, to comfort him, to help him in his hour of need. What stuck the knife in deeper was the fact that he used me to gain her sympathy. He told her things weren't good with us, that I wasn't doing enough and he was confused as to how I felt about him. WAS HE SERIOUS! By this point, I had given up friendships. I didn't go out, didn't speak to many people. My life consisted of him and university, and I was even fighting to make that work. The amount I had done for him, the amount of abuse I had taken from him, the sheer audacity he had to even say I was leaving a shadow of a doubt in his mind that I wanted to be with him. I'll bet none of this came up in their conversation though, did it?

It really is astounding how he made something that he fucked up on my fault. It really is. If I had known from the beginning that his intention was to break me down as much as he could until he looked like my best and only option, then I would have walked away. But he did it quietly. Like an animal stalking its prey. He was stealthy, he kept quiet, he pounced on vulnerability. What a kill he made! I didn't see what was coming until I was in over my head.

7.
I finally felt like we'd had a breakthrough

I didn't fall back into the relationship easily. By that, I mean I started speaking to him because I felt obligated after that voicemail he left. I felt stuck when he started to make me feel as if I was responsible for his mental welfare. He didn't so much say out loud what the outcome of me breaking off contact from him would be, but he didn't have to. I read between the lines. I knew exactly what he was implying. For a few days it was phone calls and messages constantly asking what I was going to do and a blatant disregard for the space I had asked for. His constant asking of "What are you going to do?" implied that he didn't accept that I had said I didn't want to be in the relationship anymore and made it seem like there was still a choice to be made.

In my mind it was an instant switch. I didn't want to be with somebody who could cheat on me, not again. It was that clear cut. However, over the course of the few days that followed his confession, I was worn down. I started to doubt my decision and started to ask myself whether it could be me that was partly to blame in all of this. I did care about him. I wanted to be with him and I'd already made sacrifices for the relationship to work. The doubt got big enough to warrant me going to see him the following weekend. I thought, maybe if he saw the resolve of my decision for himself then he would accept that it was over and that would be that. It was so, so much easier to be adamant in my decision when I didn't see him face-to-face, so going to see him was a huge mistake. I found it easier to take a firm stance in text messages. In person, I didn't stand a chance.

I knew I could be worn down but I went anyway because I couldn't leave the relationship feeling that I was the cause of him cheating. I would have hated him thinking I wasn't open enough or I didn't care enough. He had manipulated the whole situation to make me feel as though I still had something to prove to him. This mindset carried me to the point of feeling like being in the relationship again was him giving me another chance. Another chance to show him that not everybody in this world was set out to treat him badly. I genuinely cared for him and I loved the side of him that was so eager for us to work, the side that was comfortable and, at times, even vulnerable.

I arrived at his house on the Saturday night – the first time I had seen him since he told me about him and Sarah. He came to the door. He hadn't done this in a while – usually I would make my way through the house until I found him. It felt nice to be seen. Now, when I say the next few hours were overwhelming, that may be a slight understatement. He was the most loving and attentive he had been, ever. He waited on me hand and foot. He was telling me all the things I needed to hear, the things I had needed to hear for the entire relationship; he chose now, this moment, to give that to me. I felt relieved to have finally made some sort of breakthrough with him. It was the early hours of the morning now and we were still awake, watching a film in bed.

"You need to be honest with me." I turned to him, "If you're not happy or I'm not giving you what you need, then it's me you need to be telling." I propped myself up on my elbows and looked him in the eye.
"I promise I will. I'm sorry I never before. You were already distancing yourself, so I didn't want to scare you off by asking for too much." His eyes didn't break contact with

mine the whole time. I could feel myself melting, "It just hurt me more that you felt you couldn't come to me, but I understand. No more secrets?" I took my eyes away from his gaze and looked down at the bed, expecting a backlash for asking for so much. "No more secrets." He took his fingertips and brought my chin up until I was looking back into his eyes again. He moved my hair away from my face, and right as he was about to kiss me, he received a text, breaking the moment. "That's her" he said, so casually. His mood shifted from in-the-moment to very-much-annoyed. He locked his screen and diverted his attention back to me.
"What did she want?" I really didn't even want to know. I just couldn't think of anything else to say. I was shocked that he was honest with me.
"She's out with friends so I think she's a little bit drunk." No sooner had he said that, his phone start flashing with an incoming call. It was Sarah. I was shocked when he rejected the call. "I just want you to be able to trust me, so I'm being honest with you. I don't want to know her. It's inappropriate for us to try to be friends now." I stayed sat up on the bed, wide-eyed. I couldn't believe that he had suddenly found all of this foresight and was

able to anticipate what I might need. Still, I was glad I didn't have to *ask* him to do that. "Okay" is all I could manage before my blood started flowing properly again. "I appreciate that, I really do." I gave a satisfied smile to try and convince him that I was happy with the gesture he had just made. His phone started to ring again. This time, he jumped up off the bed, walked across the room and closed to door to as he answered his phone. "What?" I heard him snap. "Don't call me again." There was a pause and I could hear her voice telling him they needed to talk. "No we don't! Don't call me again, I said!" and he hung up the phone. "I don't want anything to ruin us," he claimed as he walked back into the room, closing the door behind him as if nothing had just happened. He made his way back over to the bed and took his place where he had been before. As he lay back down, he placed his hands on my shoulders and gently pulled me back to lie down with him. He left one arm out for me to lie on and I rested my head on his chest. That's how we stayed until we fell asleep.

The next morning, I woke up before he did. My mind was still racing over what had happened the previous night. As I lay next to him, I wondered how he could go from somebody who cheated on me, had me running round in circles and changing so much about myself and my life to this man who had displayed so much maturity without it seeming difficult at all for him. He anticipated every which way I may need reassurance and showed me that I could place confidence in him. I was so confused.

After quietening my mind from the million miles-per-hour it was racing at, I put it down to him really seeing what he was about to lose if I walked away. It was a reasonable explanation for how quickly he changed his act. It only solidified further my opinion of him being a really nice person – he was just scared of being hurt. He had a really sweet side to him. All of the outrageous requests and the way he was trying to communicate were only because he didn't know how to really communicate. He wasn't sure how to *be* in a relationship. I resolved within myself to be the one to show him what a relationship was supposed to be like. What love was supposed to be like. Love? Well, I was so hurt that he cheated; I was terrified of him hurting himself as *that* voicemail had hinted towards. I had already put so much into it. I

felt like I could bring out the good in him,
amongst other things, so yes, love.

8.
Somebody is better than nobody

In the few months prior, the tension at home between my parents and myself had become palpable. I was tired of snaking around the house, hoping I wouldn't be seen. I was constantly on edge, waiting for them to question me on who I was with, where I was going, whether I would be home that night. I had told Mum so many times that our relationship was over. Yet she knew that if he clicked his fingers, I would go running like I had so many times before. My parents had front-row seats, watching how I'd changed everything about myself and my life to cater to Aaron. They had seen the break-ups and the make-ups. They saw every inch of anxiety I was carrying around daily. I thought that if I could do a better job of hiding it, then they would be happier for me. But how could they ever be happy with me being in a relationship that demands I change everything about myself?

I told Mum I was going bowling for my birthday… *with friends*. She knew I was lying. I knew she knew I was lying. At times I would wonder why they felt the need to know every detail of my life. After all, I was 22 years old now, so why did they still treat me like I was 13? Always asking where I was going, who with, when they could expect me home and so on. It felt overbearing and, at times, too much. I never actually told them this though. I just answered their questions and hoped they didn't ask more. This was different though. They had never judged me for the company I kept or what I was doing before, but they did with Aaron. They saw something I couldn't see. They saw me diminishing in front of their own eyes and they didn't like it. I was becoming a smaller version of myself by the day and it upset them so much.

Something had changed. I felt useless on my own. I felt like I couldn't cope with being alone. He was like an addiction. I hated the fact I needed him, but it didn't erase the fact that I did need him. It had taken him just one year to completely change me as a person. Before we met, I was confident, I had a bright future, I wasn't scared to be myself, I was friendly and loved being out and about. Now? Well, now I was a mess, with reducing prospects and everything I had built myself up to be, everything I had planned, my dreams, shattered. All because he came in with a sledgehammer to get what he felt entitled to, and my entire life was just collateral damage. As long as he got what he wanted, he was happy.

So, why did I need Aaron? Why did I still love him? Why did I feel so happy whenever he would call or text? It's not like the communication between us was what I had needed or wanted to hear. It was mostly some form of insult, spiel on what I had done wrong, directions on how to make myself better – for him, not for myself, but for him. Yet this was the only thing in my life that was making me happy. In fact, I wouldn't even say happy, but it was the only thing that made me feel like I could cope with life. The only thing I was doing right and the only thing that mattered. He had spent so long breaking me down and convincing me that he was what I needed that when he took himself away from me, I felt unable to carry on. When we'd get back together and were on the right track, I knew I had my crutch back. I was convinced of his logic that if I was nothing without him, and nobody would want to be with me, then when I was with him I was 'something', right? Even if that something was really small, I was still something, and something felt better than nothing.

I got so addicted to the feeling it gave me when we made up after each break-up. It was like all the validation I needed was finally given to me. The barrage of abuse he gave when we'd break up was never worth it, *ever*. It didn't quite feel that way at the time, though. It was like every time we got back together, he would build me up, let me have some self-worth, make me feel validated and special. Then, just as easily as he gave it, he took it away. The break-ups were him pulling the rug from under my feet. He was quite happy to watch me fall, no matter the height. And I fell, every time. And every time, he would be my saviour all over again. He became my supply of everything I needed to get myself through the day. I could only have some confidence if he supplied it. I could only have some self-worth if he supplied it. I could only feel loved, respected, validated and so on if he supplied it. Was it any wonder that I felt addicted to him?

Something was becoming much more deep-rooted than needing him, though. I had spent my whole life, up until I was 19 years old, single. It didn't bother me in the slightest. I didn't want or need a boyfriend. I didn't feel like I was missing out or that I should have a boyfriend. I was truly happy on my own. Plus, I wasn't on my own – I had a handful of friends that were solid. I could rely on them for anything and I knew those friendships would last, no matter what. My family were supporting me through everything I wanted to do – and being the dreamer I was, I wanted to do it all. I wanted to get to the top of that career ladder. I wanted the expensive car. I wanted the big house. I wanted to see the sights and experience everything. My family were the ones that kept my dreams within my sight. What's more, I was actually making it happen. I had university and I was working for my own money, too. So when I thought of where a boyfriend would fit in to all of this, I knew that however it happened, it would be because I *wanted* a boyfriend in my life, not because I *needed* a boyfriend in my life.

Aaron was so good at manipulating me into giving up so much of myself that I didn't see the problem he was causing behind this. I had started to not only think that I needed him – but that I would always need *somebody*. Any time he would get abusive and tell me that nobody would want me and I wouldn't be able to ever make anybody happy, it triggered me into believing that I would always need somebody. That just maybe, I couldn't do any of it on my own as I had previously thought. He made me feel so naïve for not seeing this sooner. It was so painful for me to realise that I needed to grieve for my independence – and I did lose it. For as long as I believed that I would always *need* somebody, I would never have my independence.

9.
Divide and conquer

If I had just one wish to make for my birthday that year, it would have been for Aaron and I to get to the place that always seemed to be just outside of my reach. We had broken up (again) around five days previously, and after making up and spending New Year's Eve together, we were now at a point where, I thought, things were finally going better for us (again).

As we were sat in the bowling alley, I felt so happy that this was for me. Yet at the same time, I felt so guilty that I couldn't enjoy this without upsetting other people. Aaron had done this. He had always been convinced that my parents didn't like him – even before they had ever met him. The reality was, they didn't like what they saw me changing into; and at the centre of those changes was Aaron. So, by default, they were apprehensive about me being in this relationship. Every time something involved both Aaron and my family, I felt that a choice had to be made as to who was involved, because I could never have both.

It wasn't long before Mum was texting, asking when I would be home so we could celebrate and I could spend some time with my family on my birthday.

When do you think you will be back?

I'm not too sure yet, just having something to eat and we're booked on an alley for 3pm. Probably later this afternoon.

Who is we?

Just some friends I've come bowling with.

You're with him, aren't you? Don't lie to me, Becks. I know you're back together. I know it was him you went out with on New Year's Eve.

I did. I don't want to fall out with you over this. I just want to enjoy my birthday and I'll be home later. I wish you would understand.

I'm not falling out with you over him. I just wish you would realise what he is doing to you. He's no good for you.

Who I want to be with is my business. You don't understand him. He's been through a lot. You just don't know him as well as I do.

We are going to be together because he makes me happy. It's my choice.

If that's how you feel then maybe it's best you don't come home then. I love you Becky but I can't watch you do this to yourself.

Okay.

I could feel Aaron getting agitated by the fact that I was texting back and forth. I wanted to take my mum's opinions on board but somehow, I just felt like the slightest bit of agreement from me would be like I was betraying Aaron – and him finding *those* text messages would surely mean more leverage for him. It's not like he didn't check up on me or go through my phone. So instead of being open to what my mum was saying, I made sure that if Aaron did ask who I was texting and checked up on me that he wouldn't find something that hurt him to read.

Mum had never told me that she loved me very often. She was always one to show how she felt rather than tell. Even growing up in what I thought at the time was a strict household, I know it was my mum trying to keep my older sister and I out of harm's way. I was always the one in my friendship group that had the earliest curfew. It was always my mum asking for phone numbers of other mums to check I would be where I said I would be. Mum worked 16-hour days for years to keep the house in order and give us everything we ever needed. She was always very house proud and kept our home looking immaculate. I learnt a lot of decorating and DIY skills from her. Mum and I spent around three weeks of the summer holidays one year redecorating an apartment belonging to my great auntie. This was the first job I was ever paid for – cash-in-hand, of course. I used the money to treat myself to a brand new phone, a pink LG Cookie, and some new clothes. It was sweltering that summer and we were glistening head to toe in sweat at the end of each day, but it was so worth it. The flat was stunning when we had finished, and seeing how pleased my great auntie was with it taught me why Mum went out of her way so much to help other people.

We didn't have a lot of money growing up but it never felt that way; Mum had a way of helping us make the best of what we did have. At times, it was obvious how tired she was – a tell-tale sign of how hard she worked. She would hide away in her bedroom sometimes just to get some peace. When Mum did spend time with us, her personality was so vibrant. She was so caring, always the first to help anybody that needed it. She wasn't scared of trying new things and starting new businesses whenever it was possible. Sometimes I did crave to be told how much I meant to her, but Mum was always a very the-proof-is-in-the-pudding kind of woman. I know this has been the reason why I've always sought validation in how people behave towards me, as opposed to believing everything I was told. Aaron had told me how he felt about me; something that I craved, and yet when he did it just felt so empty. He had told me what sort of man he was and what kind of life he wanted to build for himself. I was starting to feel as though I'd hung around just a little bit too long to see whether the actions would match.

As Aaron sat and read the texts from my mum as I guessed he would, I tried my best to read his face. Was he about to offer an olive branch to my family? Would he abandon me the same way it felt Mum had just done? Would we look at working out a solution together? His face gave away nothing. As I sat nervously waiting for a reaction, I couldn't help but hope it wouldn't end in a very public argument. I was on edge, fidgeting with my hands, giving the excuse that I was cold. Eventually he gave a sigh. He looked up at me and his face had a look of concern spread across it.

"So, what are we going to do?" he said, completely taking me aback, *we*?
"I don't know. Maybe I should go home and talk to my mum. If she sees how serious we are about making us work then maybe she will warm to the idea." The best outcome would be for all of this to work itself out, allowing me to have a relationship with both him and my family. He sat back in his chair, not taking his eyes away from mine.
"Or…" He nodded his head to the side and shrugged, "you could move in with me." His eyes were fixated back on me again. I could tell he was looking for my reaction.
"What, like you mean, get our own place together?" I was feeling dizzy at how this was escalating.
"Yeah. I mean, it would be easier for you to move into my mum and dad's with me first. You know? So we can save up and get started." He made it sound so easy. Yet I couldn't help but feel a little devastated that me working things out with my family had

not even entered his mind.
"Would they even be okay with that?" I didn't know if I was really ready for this step. We had never even talked about moving in together before today. "And you? I don't want you feeling like you have to do this or it's been forced on you."
"Well, your mum has basically just kicked you out. My mum and dad wouldn't see you on the streets. And I know it's a big step for us, but it'll be fun." He slid his hands across the table and put them over mine, "So what do you think?"
"I think you're right. It'll be fun," I lied, thinking about how much I wanted to go home and talk to Mum. I turned my hands up to hold his and forced a smile. As we both stood to make our way to the bowling alley, I couldn't help but think about all of the doubts. Was this what I really wanted? Was I stuck between a rock and a hard place? Was I about to jump out of the frying pan and into the fire? I pushed them to the back of my mind and tried to enjoy the rest of our time out.

From the time between those messages from Mum and being back at his house, I had a million and one thoughts running through my head. Would Mum actually make me leave the house if I stayed with him? Could I work things out with her to help her see that I wanted this relationship? Why had he not told me to work things out with her? Was it as brutal as he made it sound and Mum was kicking me out? I just didn't know where to start. My mind was racing, but on the outside I was trying to keep things cool. I mean, we were moving in together. Maybe not in the most ideal of circumstances but it was still a big deal, right? It was still something for us to be happy about. It was so bizarre to feel like this relationship milestone was something to be happy about, yet I felt… hesitant. I didn't want to leave my parents' home off the back of an argument. I didn't want our relationship milestone to be a forced hand. Perhaps living together would mean I'd be more capable, too. Maybe it was the sign that Aaron did actually want the kind of life he said he did. Either way, everything was all set. The only thing left to do was to go and get my things from home.

10.
Time for change

Back at home, I sat on my bedroom floor alone, packing my things up ready to move. I came across a trophy I had received for 'Business Student of the Year'. A trophy that earmarked a big time for change in my life, a time for change in me. I knew I didn't want the kind of jobs I'd seen the adults in my life go through. There was nothing wrong with those jobs; they paid the bills and provided for our family but they just didn't appeal to me.

So, in September 2006, I knew I didn't want to return to college to do my second year of hairdressing – I mean, I enjoyed it and I met a lot of different and talented girls during my first year, but it just wasn't very *me*. I didn't even know who *me* was, but I was starting to learn who *me* wasn't. So it was time to branch out, try something new. With that, I enrolled on a business course. For the next two years, I would be learning about everything from balance sheets to branding, from entrepreneurship to equilibrium points. It was so out of my comfort zone; it was far beyond anything I had attempted before, but I did it, and I loved it. Not only did I do it, but in those two years I spent exploring my potential, I achieved *that* award, the highest grade possible on completing the course and conditional offers from every university I applied for. Before I started the business course, I never even dreamt I could reach something like university. It just seemed like such a far-fetched idea. I mean, I knew people who had gone to university, people from my school, people from families that made more money than mine. I just didn't ever believe I was as capable and worthy as they were. I never thought I would be at *that* sort of level. That was until it was actually happening to me.

That little glass trophy became everything I wanted. I started to see how my own potential could be realised. It helped me to see so clearly what my life could be, what I wanted it to be. I could see my options, options that I never thought I would have. I could get excited for a big future. That trophy came to symbolise everything I had achieved, and was yet to achieve. I had worked so hard to not only achieve what I did in college but also to build on myself, to better myself, to make myself somebody that I actually liked. That trophy sat on the windowsill in my bedroom at my parents' house and served as my daily reminder to go and fulfil my potential. The trophy itself is a good-sized diamond shape sat on top of a block, all glass with a frosted star in the centre of the diamond and a silver plaque on the block engraved with the words 'Aim Higher Business Student of the Academic Year 2006–2007'.

It served as a reminder that, for what felt like a very rare occasion in my life, somebody chose me. Of all the students and all the work the college saw that year, it chose me. On the sunny days, the sunlight would hit the diamond and send colour spectrum flashes all over my walls and ceiling. I would sit and stare, daydreaming about where I could go next, where my life would be in the next five years, ten years, 20 years, the career heights I could reach. At this period of time in my life, I had everything I wanted, and I was content.

Everything I owned – clothes, makeup, coursework – was now all sat in black bags ready to leave my home. I had a knot in my stomach so big that I was sure it could be seen from the outside. I always knew leaving my parents' home was going to be hard, but this was on another level. I didn't want to leave in the way it was happening. I didn't feel ready for this step. Not in my relationship, not in my life in general. The knot in my stomach grew bigger with every step I took down the stairs and towards the door. I stopped in the dining room where I could see Mum sat in the living room, as downstairs was all open-plan, and my stepdad, Peter, was in the kitchen washing up. It took me a good few moments to even be able to look Mum in the face, and when I did I really wish I hadn't. I could see the pain in her expression like it was written in big, bold words. It was like looking at a reflection of what my gut was trying to tell me. I couldn't find any words to fit the moment, so I tried to keep it in tone with this being a normal, everyday kind of conversation.

"I'll text you tomorrow or something." Saying this caused an awkward silence as I looked slowly towards my mum.
She hesitated before responding, "Okay." It looked as if she wanted to say so much more but was biting her tongue.
"Our door is always open, Becks," said Peter, without turning himself away from the kitchen sink. I could feel the lump in my

throat forming. "You do know that don't you?"
"Yeah, I know." I managed to get it out before the lump swallowed my voice completely.

I didn't want to leave the home that was built on Mum's constant reminders of how much I was loved. In that moment, those reminders seemed like very distant memories. I kept on thinking, "If these walls could talk…" but I knew they couldn't, and neither could Mum. Having Mum unable to speak to me took me back to the feeling I used to get in the pit of my stomach as a child when she would stop speaking to me. Whether it was anger, disappointment or something else, the silence would send me into turmoil. I used to spend so much energy and effort trying to gain the love I never heard come out of her mouth. Always chasing something that was just out of my reach.

No tears. No hugs. No goodbyes. Nothing. I wanted Mum to tell me not to go. I wanted her to say the complete opposite of what Aaron had been saying for the past year. I wanted her to tell me I was worth more, that I deserved better and I didn't need to feel so responsible for him. I needed somebody, anybody, to tell me that. Instead, I let it all hang in the air – my silent begging for confirmation that he was wrong about me.

I picked up all the bags I had and headed out the patio door to where I'd parked the car, beyond the gate at the bottom of the back garden. I fought every urge I had to look back to where I left everything unsaid. I didn't want to look back and feel like I was on the outside looking in. This is where I had always been 'in'. This had always been my home. This is where I felt loved, safe, validated. This place was a part of me and I was a part of this place. These people were my people. My heart was at home here. I knew if I looked back as an outsider looking in, then I never would have had the strength to walk away. Maybe I should have looked back. Instead, I kept putting one foot in front of the other, loaded my bags into the boot of the car and drove the 7–8-minute drive to Aaron's house.

11.
Out of control with no safety net

"You really don't need to be spending that much time in the library, or is that just an excuse for where you really are?" Aaron said to me. The sternness in his face was scalding.
"No – I'm actually at the library. That's the level of work that is expected of me. I need to put the hours in." I got so defensive, as his accusation was so predictable yet it still got my back up every time he said it.
"But that would mean I'd barely ever see you. I have friends at uni that don't put that much time into their work." I could hear in his voice he was getting more pressing in a bid to stop me defending myself as he stood up and started to pace the bedroom. But I wasn't giving up easily.
"It all builds up with lectures and workshops and studying in the library. Plus, I'm now behind on assignments. I need to get all my work done." The pressure of having to explain myself and justify why I needed time at uni was getting unbearable. I felt so angry that I had to give a reason and explain myself for wanting to do this.
"Well, I guess that shows where your

priorities lie doesn't it!" He started to make his way to bed, leaving me stood in the living room. I could feel the room starting to spin. "I just wish I had known I'd be second best before we came this far," he said so callously as he reached the bottom of the stairs.
"You're still a priority to me." I trailed behind him hoping that my reassurance would help, or at least avoid the argument. "You knew when we met that I was at uni and studying. I thought you understood what I needed to do." As he reached the bedroom, he stopped dead in his tracks, turned his body and looked me square in the eye. I froze, in a mixture of panic and anticipation, near to the top of the stairs. I gripped the hand rail tighter.
"I suppose we best just call it a day then. It's probably for the best anyway if you're going to London." And with that he turned away from me and started to make his way to the bedroom.
"I told you I've already declined the placement after we had that conversation about it. It wasn't what was best for us. I'm going to find a placement here so we can still be together." I tried to hold back at how annoyed I was at the prospect that I could have just thrown away the best opportunity I

could have hoped for in a bid to save our relationship. That wound was very much still exposed.
"You shouldn't have bothered," he said whilst taking his clothes off beside the bed, his voice as cold as anything. "Obviously this whole uni thing is the most important thing to you. Like I said, I just wish you hadn't wasted my time and let me fall for you." I couldn't respond to what he was saying. He was forcing me into making a choice I shouldn't have had to make. I didn't want to have to make this decision, because I knew the result would be me losing another part of myself that I wanted desperately to cling on to. So I stayed silent.

Honestly, I wasn't shocked. I'd been expecting him to throw this in my face; but for the first time, I was disappointed. Not in him, but in myself because I could feel uni slipping away from me, and instead of being one of the people who jumps into action in a crisis, I was a bystander just watching the devastation unfold in front of me. All because I was too scared of the repercussions of doing something that was good for *me*, not us, just *me*. I'd already given up my industry placement at IBM. Aaron instantly squashed that idea with a whole list of reasons why we wouldn't work long-distance. How difficult it would be for him to visit me in London because he can't drive and I'd be abandoning him if I were to go. The opportunity to gain a year of experience with one of the biggest tech companies on the planet before I graduated and I turned it down.

I was exhausted. I couldn't carry on as we were. Something had to give. It was so late and I needed to go to sleep. I'd be up in a few hours for uni. We'd been arguing again. The arguments were getting more intense and more abusive. My eyes were raw from crying. Aaron had given up a few hours ago and had been sound asleep without a care in the world. My chest felt so heavy, the weight pushing down on me made me feel like I was suffocating. I sobbed until I couldn't catch my breath and began to panic. The conversation we had a few hours earlier was ringing in my ears.

"I can't cope anymore. I need to quit uni." I couldn't believe I was saying this out loud. I'd worked for this for so long, long before Aaron came on the scene. I used my sleeve to wipe the tears away from my cheeks.
"What makes you say that?" The disinterest

in his voice was so evident it was infuriating. "The workload, the travelling back and forth. I feel like I've not got enough time to catch up. I'll never find another placement now either." I was desperate for him to hear how much I wanted this. But his response was like a knife going through my chest.
"Well, if that's what you want, then that's what you should do." No emotion, at all.

NO, IT'S NOT WHAT I WANT! This was the corner Aaron had backed me into. The mind games he played had me coming to a crossroads of having to make a choice. He never once offered support or asked if there was anything he could do to help me. All he ever did was constantly call or text when I was at the library or in lectures. He wanted to know where I was constantly. He wanted to know why I would be taking so long. He always wanted to know who I was speaking to, even the slightest correspondence. I didn't speak to many people anymore. He had a way of making me feel so transparent. Like he could see right through me. This, combined with the way he would make me feel like rubbish for even saying hello to anybody else, was the exact reason it was so much easier to just avoid speaking to anybody, if I could. I felt so restricted.

I asked myself whether these kinds of questions Aaron fired at me non-stop were normal? Was this what a healthy relationship looked like? We'd agreed to be open and honest, and I had every intention of being, but this was too much. There is a fine line between being open and honest and having my own privacy. It seemed he wanted the latter to be non-existent.

I don't know why I expected Aaron to be any form of support at all. It's not as if he had a track record of making life experiences easier for me; he just used them as opportunities to shrink me down. He had no intention of easing the pressure. If anything, he turned the pressure up to boiling point so I had no choice but to make a choice. My whole life was veering off the path I'd worked hard to put it on so fast I didn't know how to stop it. In all honesty, I was terrified of trying to stop it. So, instead, I clung to him in the hope that when it all ground to a halt, he would be there to help me pick up the pieces.

12.
The top of the career ladder, which I'd been working so hard to climb, was within reach, and I jumped off

Ever since I had met Aaron in January of the previous year, uni had become a whole lot harder. I don't just mean the logistics of it – the travel back and forth did take up a lot of time every day but I'd always managed. The part of my mental capacity that I used to deal with uni before was now being consumed by him. I was trying my best to still put everything that I could into something I had been building for years, at the same time as trying to make the relationship work. He was not only jealous of the relationships I had with other people; he was also jealous of the relationship I had with myself. He was jealous that something was taking my time and attention away from him. He was jealous that I was on the right track to building something really good for myself.

We'd had so many arguments over me being at uni and needing time to put into my education. Each and every time it came to the same conclusion. The argument that we had earlier that night had been no different.

I was devastated when I declined the IBM placement offer. I thought Aaron was being honest and vulnerable with me when he said he'd be so upset if I left him and went to London. I didn't want to be the one to let him down, to let us down. He was quite happy to unload that responsibility of making us work onto my shoulders. That responsibility was an all-consuming, heavy load. The consequences of me jumping through his hoops were heavier than I ever could have anticipated; it cost me so much of myself.

My chest felt like it was going to cave in on me at any moment. I didn't have a dry part of my t-shirt to wipe my tears on anymore. I was tired of crying. I was tired of everything I did not being good enough. I was tired of all the good things in my life being tainted and having to feel guilty for having what I had worked so hard for. In the end, I decided that bowing out was better than completely failing, because in a situation where I couldn't win, no matter what I did, that's what I was headed for – failure. I wanted so much for him to be the man I knew he could be. The one that was kind and caring and thoughtful. The one that had put up with me getting things wrong from the beginning. In a way, I owed it to him to try harder, or so I thought. I felt so sick at the idea of uni not being in my life anymore, my career ending before it had even began. I had built up this whole image of how my life would play out and a successful career was a huge part of that image. I didn't jump off the ladder; I felt like I'd slipped and fallen off that ladder and hit every rung on the way down.

I knew what I had to do and every part of me was screaming not to do it. I picked up my Blackberry. Between my hand shaking and my eyes being so full with tears, I could barely see what I was doing or hit the right keys. I put it back down on the floor in front of where I was knelt at the foot of the bed. I tried to take a deep breath, hoping I could regain some control over my trembling body. I cleared my throat and wiped away my tears on the body of an already-wet t-shirt. I picked up my phone again, unlocked it and accessed my emails.

To: Zoe

From: Rebecca

Date: February 2011

Subject: Withdrawal from BA(Hons) Marketing course

Dear Zoe,

It is with a heavy heart I regret to inform you that due to personal circumstances I will be taking a step back from my studies on your BA(Hons) Marketing course. I feel the sheer workload of the course is having a substantial effect on my situation at home and I cannot complete the course to the best of my abilities at this time.

Kind regards,

Rebecca
Student, BA(Hons) Marketing

Another piece of me gone.

I curled up on the floor where I was knelt. I brought my knees to my chest and wrapped my arms around them. I sobbed uncontrollably until I fell asleep.

The worst part of quitting uni was trying to keep the fact hidden from Mum and Peter. I knew exactly what they would say. I wanted to believe they were wrong. Them saying it out loud and being right would make me have to face a reality that I felt incapable of facing.

So I kept it from them for a few months. That way I could justify my choice, because Aaron's insecurities would have eased and we would be happier; I just had to wait it out. I couldn't just tell them that quitting uni was a good idea, especially when I didn't believe it myself. I had to be able to show them it was, just like I had to be shown it was.

The one person who has always been able to read me like a book Peter. Growing up, if I ever did anything to get myself into trouble, or I knew Mum wouldn't be happy with, I could always turn to Peter for help. He was always very laid back and had a logical approach to everything. It balanced out Mum's emotional approach and is probably one of the reasons why they worked so well together, like a yin and yang.

I was 16 years old when I got into trouble – resulting in a criminal record. One of my high-school best friends had a chip on her shoulder about another girl that had been touting racial slurs at her younger sister. One night, when we were out in the part of the town where my best friend lived, we saw the car that this girl had been going to school in. My best friend and I did enough damage to result in the car being written off. I'd always been a fast runner – PE was my favourite lesson in my younger years at school and I'd always been good at sprint racing and netball. This probably attributed to why I managed to outrun the owner of the car that night. I couldn't escape completely though – my best friend got caught, so I had to hand myself in. Before that, I had to tell my parents what I'd done and why I needed them to come to the police station with me.

The obvious choice for me was to tell Peter first. He knew exactly what to do. We told Mum together. Peter then came to the police station with me. He asked the police officers that interviewed me to be as harsh as possible in their questioning – to scare me into not doing anything like this again. It worked! After seeing how terrified I was throughout the whole ordeal, my parents knew I had learnt my lesson. How he worked the situation from start to finish is testament to the kind of person Peter is and the kind of relationship we had. He knew just the right way to work the process to make sure I didn't dare make the same mistake twice – and I haven't.

I couldn't stomach the idea of telling Peter that I had made another mistake that would have a huge impact on my life. He had been my reassurance whenever I had doubt. He had been my practical help when I needed help. He had been my support whenever it got too much emotionally. He had been my financial support, as much as he could have, wherever I fell short. He had invested so much into me getting to the point of having so much to throw away. He had helped me climb the rungs of the ladder. There was no way I could tell him that I'd jumped off near the top without anything substantial to show for it. I knew it would tear him to pieces, just as much as I knew he would understand more than anybody how much it had torn me to pieces.

13.
It was a car crash – my nerves, the relationship, everything

On the face of things, we were doing well. When it came to making plans together, we were making good progress. I had found a job in a call centre. Not exactly a high-flying marketing career like I had been on track for the previous year, but it paid the bills and allowed us to start saving enough money to get our own place. It helped me to feel like even though I had given up a lot, I was also still capable of something; I still held some form of value even if it wasn't as much as before. Now that we had money coming in to help us on our way, I hoped it would ease the tensions between us. Stress had become Aaron's go-to excuse for how abusive he was.

I'd be burdened with a lot of the blame as to why we were stuck in a rut. It was always my fault that things weren't going right for him. I thought that if I could provide income for us to be able to move forward together, it would ease some of the stress for Aaron. Working also brought on new tensions that I didn't anticipate – but probably should have going off experience. Whenever I would walk to or from work, I was on the phone to Aaron. I thought this was sweet and sensible in the beginning, as he always played it off as a safety thing. He was, in fact, checking to make sure I wasn't walking to and from work with anybody else. He would question whether I had made friends with anybody at work and tried to use one of my colleagues who he happened to know from childhood football clubs to check up on me.

The tensions manifested in different ways. It was as if we just *couldn't* be happy. He would always find something new to become an issue. The fights were exhausting, extensive and he always had to have the last word. I had learnt over time that it was much safer for me to take the blame for whatever it was I was being blamed for. If I ever questioned what he was saying or tried to suggest he take accountability for his wrongdoing, it was always met with a barrage of abuse detailing everything I had ever done wrong.

I had started to go back to my parents' house after arguments got too much. I'd play it off as just a visit or popping in as I was walking by, but I think they knew I just needed an escape. The first time I went back home to my parents' following one of these arguments was when Aaron's lack of thought for consequence became very obvious. As we drove back home after shopping, he made it very obvious he wasn't happy with the amount of money the food shop had cost. *Something as basic as us eating to live.* He had other plans for the money we had, and it had created an inconvenience for him because now he had to source money for gambling from elsewhere.

"It wasn't even necessary for us to spend so much money," Aaron barked as we drove towards the bridge.
"What else are we supposed to do? It's cheaper than spending money on takeaways every night. It means we'll be able to save up quicker," I responded, knowing full well any explanation I gave wouldn't suffice.
"It would be quicker if you had more hours at work. We need more money, not cutting costs." He was now sat with his back straight, raising his voice through gritted teeth as we cornered the bend after the bridge.
"I can't do more hours until work open up some overtime." I could feel the tension rising and tried to concentrate on the road.
"NO. You just won't do more hours because

you're lazy. You think it's perfectly fine to live at my mum and dad's house forever because it's easier for you. If you were a bit less bone idle then maybe we'd actually be somewhere by now."
"It's not easy living at your parents' house at all. I don't want to be living under somebody else's roo—"
"WATCH OUTTT"

The car skidded on oil that had been spilled on the road. Before I could do anything about it, we had spun backwards and were headed straight for the embankment lined with trees. I heard a huge bang synchronised with the sound of glass smashing. I could hear my heartbeat in my ears and I flushed head to toe with heat. When the car had finally stopped still, I was frozen, for what felt like days. I couldn't even comprehend where I was or what I was doing. Out of nowhere this voice came across.

"What the fuck do you think you're doing?" The first and only thing Aaron shouted in my face, snapping my senses back to reality.

I couldn't answer even if I wanted to. I was shell-shocked. Unhurt, but shell-shocked. I looked over to see Aaron staring at me with a face of thunder. I couldn't see any injuries on him. He opened his door and started walking towards a car that had pulled over just up ahead to check if we were okay. As my senses returned to my body, I could see that he was telling the gentleman that had pulled over that we were okay and didn't need any help. I didn't even know if that was true. I felt in no fit state to drive. I couldn't even make sense of what had just happened, how we had ended up entangled in the trees with no rear window, a wing mirror missing and my nerves in tatters on the side of the expressway. I didn't have a clue what to do in this kind of situation. I didn't know if we had to call somebody, if we needed to clear up the debris. I hadn't long passed my driving test and they really didn't tell you what to do in this kind of situation. After the gentleman reluctantly left, Aaron made a short phone call. He then got back in the passenger side, brushing away the broken glass in the process.

"Drive us home," he snapped at me. I could hear the restraint in his voice.
"But I don't even know if I'm supposed to be driving now, if the car is even driveable." On top of the shock, I started to run these

questions through my mind, realising this situation could be a huge mess for us to clear up.
"I said…" He turned and looked me straight in the eye, "Drive. Us. Home." My stomach dropped as he snapped at me.
"O… okay," I stammered and started the engine, checked what was left of the mirrors and pulled away from the shredded mess that was the embankment at the side of the expressway.

This wasn't like me. I thought I had done a good job of learning how to not let Aaron's rants and abuse get to me. I thought my shell was hardening up and becoming impenetrable. All of the time I had spent putting my wall up brick by brick was for nothing, because in those few moments before the car had slipped on the road, he managed to knock it all down.

I had gone for what felt like years without arguing back. I'd tried so hard not to say or do anything that would provoke a reaction, because Aaron was reactive. Anytime he told me I had to change, that I had done something wrong, that I was the one that needed him, that I had upset him, that I was acting or speaking out of line and he was abusive as a result, it was always, *always* because *I* had done something and *he* was reacting. Never acting, always reacting. I had initiated his behaviour somehow each and every time. He never took accountability for his own actions, because, according to him, he never had any *actions* to take accountability for. I had spent the past few months walking on eggshells trying to make sure I didn't say or do anything to trigger an abusive episode. It was the safest way for me to live day-to-day. A survival technique that had become my default. I thought I was doing so well, until today. He had spent the past 17 months scrutinising my every move so I was now convinced that *I* was the problem.

I can't even remember getting home. My mind was frozen at the sight of the crash. I may as well have been one of the branches that took the weight of the car and was left a wreck on the embankment. I was full of the weight of the world, not the whole world but my world – and Aaron's. I was now so consumed by this life of trying to manage daily with not only carrying the weight of my load, but carrying his weight too. I felt as though I was suffocating with the lack of being able to stop and catch my breath even for a second. The fog had been so thick for so long that I hadn't noticed just how much weight I was bearing. I needed to get out. I needed to take a step back and let my own thoughts catch up with me. I needed time out to switch off my autopilot and process just exactly what the past 16 months had meant to me, what it had done. So that night, I went and stayed back at Mum's house – I went back home.

14.
Upping the ante

As I sat on the couch in my mum's living room, I felt something that I hadn't felt for so many weeks. I felt safe. I needed this. The whole of the relationship was starting to piece together, and it looked something like the aftermath of what had happened earlier that day. It was me – I was the crash. I still couldn't believe that I had lost control like I did. The past few weeks had me so unravelled. I had a gut feeling there was so much more to it but I couldn't quite put my finger on what it was. I just felt so uncomfortable with my reality. I'd started to see Aaron and the whole relationship in a different light. The more I sat and thought about it with the freedom to do so – no interruptions, no outside input, no him – the more I started to get a clear picture of what was happening around me, happening to me.

I had become so disattached from everything I was before. There were still parts of my life that were present. But they weren't quite part of my life. It was almost like I was being confined by an electric fence. It was stopping me from seeing, feeling, touching the parts of me that I wanted to keep close. Anytime I tried to reach outside the fence, I'd get a sharp shock. The shock served as a reminder that I should keep to the parts of my life that the fence – that was Aaron – allowed. The physical pain of the electric shocks was no more dissimilar to the emotional and mental pain of seeing my life that I couldn't quite have as a part of me anymore. Aaron was now a filter in my life and everything had to go through him. If he didn't like what was being filtered, it got discarded. He was finding it too easy to discard parts of me. I didn't quite recognise who or what this filtered version of me was, or what I was supposed to do about it.

My emotions had got the better of me on a few occasions. I had acted so out of character during a few arguments that I didn't even recognise the person I was anymore. My thoughts of self-hate were getting so out of control it scared me. I couldn't help but feel there must be something I was missing. I was completely missing something that was right in front of me and I just didn't know how to look directly at it – or what I was looking at when I did. I was too scared to look directly at it. Too scared that one realisation could unravel my whole life as I knew it at this point. I knew exactly what I had to do; I knew I had to deal with the consequences of my own actions from the past few months. I had to start taking responsibility.

"Mum, can I ask a favour?" I managed to get it out.
"Sure, what it is?" I could already see the thoughts racing through her mind.
"Can you take me to a shop? I think I need to go and get a pregnancy test." I'm surprised she heard me as I could barely get the words out. It was met by a long silence. I could tell that Mum was hoping I wasn't. Not because she wouldn't like me to become a mother at some point, just not now, not like this, not with Aaron.
"Come on then. I suppose we need to find out one way or another." She responded as she got up and walked towards the hallway to get her shoes on.

Forty-five minutes later and we were back at home, and the only thing I had left to do was to pee on this stick. This stick that looked so harmless yet held the power to completely change everything within three minutes.

Did I want to be a mum? No. I'd never contemplated what it would be like to have children. I had no desire to find out. What I did want was a career. I wanted all of those possibilities that I had discovered through college to materialise. I was still grieving for my education that had been ripped away from me. I should have fought harder for it. I should have fought harder to keep that part of me, with me. I wanted to travel; I had barely seen the world, and with the doors that had opened for me in the years previous, I couldn't wait to get out there and see it all. I had missed one or two opportunities to venture further afield; I didn't want to miss any more. I wanted to walk on the hot, sandy beaches of the Maldives, ride on the gondolas in Venice, soak in the mystery of Egypt's pyramids, experience the cultures and different ways of life of the Greek islands, see the rainbow mountains in Peru. I wanted to see it all, and having the freedom to do that felt a million miles away when adding a baby into the mix.

Of course, it's not impossible, but the whole aspect of motherhood I felt was so far from who I was and what qualities of life I valued most – freedom, independence, flexibility.

Could I really turn my back on the life I had envisioned for myself for a life that was the polar opposite? Did I have it in me to be a mother? Could I give a baby everything it would need and want? I couldn't even keep a grown man happy and control my life at the moment. What chance would I have of nurturing a tiny human that would be depending fully on me to provide everything it needed. Even if, by some very small chance, I could adapt to a life of motherhood and alter my life's course to now be 'me plus one' instead of just me, would I 100% be able to fill that role anyway?

I had made a complete mess of my own life and lost so much already. How could I even begin to believe I could be a good mother? I had somebody in my life that I loved and cared for, and he was still so unhappy. It wasn't enough for him. What chance did I have of being enough for an infant that would be completely relying on me to provide stability, safety, love. I was totally lacking in that right now. I couldn't even show the man I loved that I loved him. Something that is supposedly so natural and just falls into place when it's right is how the fairy tale goes, and I couldn't even manage that. I felt so scared, I felt unready, I felt blindsided by this and I didn't know what to do. The only thing I could do in that moment was find out whether these were questions that needed answering. So, pee stick in hand, I went to the bathroom to wait for three-felt-like-a-lifetime-minutes to find out whether the narrative I had set out for my life was about to be changed completely.

"Well… What does it say?" Mum barely let me reach the bottom of the stairs before she wanted to know. I made my way through to the living room to join Peter, Mum trailing behind closely.
"It says… it says I'm pregnant." I could barely believe the words that were coming out of my own mouth as they fell into a silent room. "What do I do now?"
"You do what you feel is best for *you,* Becky." It felt like this was an order coming from Mum, rather than advice.
"Whatever you do decide to do, we're with you 100%. You won't be doing any of this alone," added Peter in a voice of concern that sounded so familiar.
"Just know that whatever you do decide to do, it is a commitment that both you and Aaron will be making for the rest of your

lives, together. Whether you want it to be or not." At this point, I could tell that Mum's overriding thought was me.

I knew exactly what Mum was getting at. She was trying to warn me that no matter what happened between Aaron and I from that point forward, there would be no clean break if either of us decided to call it a day. We would never be able to fully walk away from each other. I would always be tied to him and he would always be tied to me. As long as there was a human being walking this planet that was half of him and half of me, we would always be connected. I was fully aware that my parents didn't think he was the right person for me and if we had a child together, then there was no chance of me fully escaping him.

Deep down I thought the real issue we had at the moment was him blaming me for everything, relentlessly. But those two lines on that little white stick made me question whether I had been out of line. My hormones had been making me feel so sensitive that my reactions were exacerbating the tense situations we often found ourselves in. Aaron hated me showing emotion and it felt like lately that's all I was capable of even though I was trying my best to bottle it up. At times I felt robotic, like I was outside of my own body watching myself, rather than being in the moment. It certainly explained why I couldn't keep myself in check earlier that day when I lost control of the car. It took me all evening to convince myself that now I knew what the issue was, I knew what to do to fix it. We could now pinpoint where all of the problems were coming from. We could work together to find the best way forward, as a family. Aaron and I would now have to work *together* on a combined goal – raising our child.

15.
It's amazing, sometimes, how rapidly things can change

I didn't recognise myself anymore. I had changed so much since Aaron and I had moved in together. Physically, my body was going through changes that I just hadn't anticipated. I mean, I knew what pregnancy does to a woman but to actually experience the relentlessness of it was a whole different kind of level of understanding. I felt nauseous all day. It was never-ending and made worse anytime that I moved. I was tired – of course I was. I was growing another human life inside of me. I was coming home from work desperate to go to sleep just to try and claw back some of the energy I needed to keep myself going. I suffered with migraines that were so debilitating. I found it so difficult to adjust to the constant discomfort. My body was growing in ways it never had before and I had to just go with it.

I had changed a lot mentally, too. I found my thought processes were a lot more complicated than they were before. I had to second guess whether everything I said or did would provoke an episode of rage from

Aaron. I knew I was physically exhausted and that was to be expected. What I didn't expect was to be mentally exhausted. I felt this constant fog over my brain and I struggled with even the simplest of thought processes. It was like I was stranded at sea in thick fog and I needed a lighthouse to guide me. Only the lighthouse never appeared and I was just constantly adrift with no idea which way shore was or how to get there. I was living in a constant state of playing catch-up with him. Our daily lives became a constant cycle of him finding a reason for his rage and me trying to figure out what I had to do to fix the situation or change something to make him happy. It was happening so fast and so often, I felt like I could never catch up. The sea was never calm and I was running out of energy to weather the storm.

The easiest way for me to keep things moving forward was to concentrate on getting everything ready for the baby. We needed a place of our own to live; we needed everything for the baby – a pram, a car seat, a cot, clothes etc. The pressure of what was to come had started building and I was so terrified, as I really didn't know what I was doing. I was going to appointments to check in with my midwife and not knowing what to ask. I had no idea there were so many choices around pregnancy, labour, birth and beyond. One of the most difficult parts was going to these appointments alone and not knowing how to answer questions. This was partly because of the brain fog, and I didn't have the mental capacity to do the research around what choices were available to me. I felt like nothing was sinking in even when I did try to read up on the best choices I could make. It was also partly because Aaron wasn't at these appointments with me for the majority of the time. I felt that if I made a decision alone, then he would accuse me of not including him. If I had taken the initiative to do what was best for me and/or the baby, then I felt that in some way I would get it wrong. I was stuck between a rock and a hard place. I was too scared to even ask him to make sure he was there for appointments so that he could have the opportunity to be more involved.

With the way things were going, the more the pregnancy advanced, the more outrageous Aaron's behaviour was getting. By this point I was well and truly walking on eggshells. I constantly watched everything I was saying and doing, trying to choose everything I said and did based on what the safest outcome would be for me. I felt so guilty for having a job. I was getting up and going out to work five days a week. I was the only one of us bringing in any form of income. I was trying to budget for a house and buying everything we needed. Yet, somehow, I felt guilty, like I wasn't doing enough.

It was eating away at me that I was given this opportunity to provide, whereas Aaron was sat at home seemingly feeling awful about himself and the fact that he was struggling to get a job and provide the same. He was being so hard on himself for not being able to find the 'right' job and contribute towards us setting our family up on the right track. The only thing he was doing was gambling, heavily. I didn't believe for a second when he said that he was doing it for our benefit, that him chasing that big win would pay off. That once he caught a lucky break it would all be worth it – it was just safer for me not to protest. Not only was my job supporting us and our unborn child, it was also financing Aaron's addiction that had unfolded and revealed just how out of control it was recently. I was struggling so much to try and keep up with everything that things were slipping, and I didn't see his problem for what it was until I'd been pulled into it with him as his enabler. I was struggling, so much so that it had started to become apparent to the people around me too.

"Do you know why I've called this meeting?" my manager asked as we sat down alone in a secluded room.
"I do," I responded. I couldn't tell whether the sick feeling was morning sickness or nerves.
"I need to explain to you how we handle lateness here and the disciplinary process we have to go down once the issue of lateness reaches a certain point." Oh God, this was it! I was about to be dismissed.
"Okay…" I held my breath for the next part.
"Looking at the reasons you've given for previous occasions and the reason you've given here today, is there anything you'd like to talk about?" I managed to breathe out just a little when I heard a pang of concern in her voice.
"No, I'm just really stressed out at the moment and I can't sleep, so I'm late getting to work. I'm struggling with trying to find a house for us and getting everything ready for the baby." I had so much more I was

struggling with, but I stopped at that.
"It can be awful, I know. Is there nothing more to it than that? If there is, you can speak to me in confidence, Becks, off the record. I can help you." My manager had a very motherly vibe to her, which was one of the reasons why she was so well-liked amongst our team.
"No, it's just that… I'm really sorry. I won't be late again." I was hoping that would be enough but it clearly wasn't.

My manager saw right through the ridiculous excuses I had just given her. It was like she could smell the truth on me. To be blunt, I had no idea what I thought she could help with but this was because I wasn't aware of the extent of my situation myself. I didn't understand. Being in the thick of the situation, my attention was drawn to the details. All of the little excuses, the blame, the circumstances, the awful behaviour from him. I could justify it all on an individual basis. Being in the centre of it all, it was so hard for me to step outside of it and see the bigger picture for what it was. None-the-less, I obviously felt the need to hold back on what was really going on. That damn gut feeling telling me that if I were to be honest about our relationship, people would serve me a few home truths that I just wasn't ready to hear.

I didn't want my manager to cast Aaron in a bad light or assume he was an awful person, because I believed he wasn't. Aaron had genuine problems that he needed help with – real, professional help. I had come to this realisation recently and the only thing it did was make me feel more tied to him, more responsible for him. I felt if I opened up to anybody and told them what was going on, then I would have to explain why this relationship was worth fighting for. I just didn't have the energy or brain capacity to be doing that right now. So it was easier to keep quiet.

16.
The last little piece

I was only 45 minutes into the exact same shift that I had that meeting with my manager when the texts started rolling in. It was unusual for Aaron to be up and out of bed so early in the day. My heart sank to the bottom of my stomach. Call it intuition, it could have been the climax of the past few days, or maybe I just knew what to expect from him now, like he had become predictable and his behaviour was starting to show the same patterns. Whatever it was, I knew what those texts were going to say. And I was right. And I was devastated!

Beck, I'm so sorry.

What for?

I didn't mean to. I was doing so well. And I lost it all.

My laptop is broken, isn't it?

Yeah, it'll probably need a new screen. It's smashed.

Okay

Okay! OKAY? It was not okay. Not even a little bit. I didn't even know where to start! Maybe the part where Aaron had been up until the early hours of the morning the night before because he was gambling? Shouting and smashing things up whenever he lost – which was often! Or the part where he had purposely waited up until midnight for *my* wages to clear into *my* bank account so he could gamble that away too. I knew he had lost my whole month's wage, a whole month's worth of *my* hard work in less than three hours last night, so I didn't even want to ask where the money had come from for this morning's episode. Yes, all of that was reason enough for me to walk away.

But… that laptop. The very first expensive thing I ever bought for myself, with my own hard-earned money, to set myself up for university. It was the first step of what I was going to do for myself and my life. It meant so much to me. And I mean, insane amounts of sentimental value, and he just bulldozed through it like it was nothing. Yes, I was so angry over all of the other stuff, but the fact that he had, quite literally, smashed all my hard work, and the value I had put into it, to pieces. That's the part that hit me in the gut and knocked the wind right out of me.

I bought that laptop with the money I had earned cleaning offices every evening after college. Quite literally after college – we never had a PC or laptop at home; Mum and Peter just couldn't afford it at the time. So, I'd stay late at college so I could use the computers in the library and then go straight to work cleaning offices – my first ever job. Me and three others, cleaning two office floors plus toilets and the canteen in two hours every evening. It wasn't a bad job. It paid the money that I needed to start my driving lessons and get myself ready for university. It was a local job, just a short walk to and from home, but in the winter months, Mum would pick me up, as she didn't want me walking alone in the dark. I didn't mind walking but she insisted. I was never too proud to admit that I was cleaning for a living. Peter had managed to pay his mortgage and provide everything we needed growing up when he cleaned at a local factory for a living. If it was good enough for him and our family, then it was good enough for me too. It was never my long-term goal. It was a stepping stone I needed to fund the longer-term goals I had set for myself.

The office floors were huge. Desks full of phones and computers. Some of the office staff had personalised their desks with photo frames. It was nice to see so many people that thought of their loved ones throughout the day. I often wondered what kind of life I would have outside of work. I knew I'd love to travel more than I had, which was barely.

There was one office that I loved to clean, because it was the one office I could see myself working in, in a similar role as the occupant of that office. It wasn't on the main floor with all the other cubicles, it was set to the side and private. I always daydreamed what it would be like to be a big boss of a multi-million-pound food distribution company, or a big boss of anything for that matter. This boss had his family photos set on his desk like the rest of the staff did. A spacious office with a big leather chair facing the door. His computer was more up to date than the others in the office. What I found myself marvelling at for longer than I probably should have was the collection of car models he had set out on the bookcase leaning flush against the wall to the right of the desk – Aston Martins, Ferraris, Lamborghinis, Porsches and the like. Always the supercars – I loved cars. I wasn't good with the ins and outs of the mechanics but I knew one car from the next and when it came to the cars that were aesthetically pleasing, I could tell you which car was which. I never did see my dream car perched on his shelf – some all-American muscle – the 1967 Mustang. Now that I would have been impressed by! That was the car I had set my sights on for when I was making good money; you don't see many classic American cars in England. In the meantime, funding my baby steps was good enough, and this job was good enough.

It took me months to save for that laptop but value meant nothing to Aaron! Yeah, sure, everything had a price tag but it didn't matter to him because his parents took care of that. Even the price he had paid in the past for his own mistakes. I often wondered why they did this. Why would they not let him learn his lessons and grow from his mistakes? Uncovering the truth, it became pretty clear why – they were scared of him. Aaron's fits of rage started long before I came onto the scene. He had even gone as far as attacking his dad in the past; pinning him to the wall by his throat. He had also been arrested for "hitting his niece" in Aaron's own played-down words. The charges were later dropped by his niece; I could take a good guess as to how that came about. Value. Sentiment. These words were alien to him. '*Okay*'? It was far from okay! But I had made the mistake of placing my loyalty in everything I had already given. I didn't think of the price of everything I was yet to give. I was being loyal to everything I had already lost without the foresight of what more I had to lose. I didn't think I had much else left to lose.

17.
Another side of me

My nerves were shattered. My head was throbbing and I could hear my heartbeat pulsing through my ears. There Aaron was, stood over me as I was sat, curled up with my knees to my chest, my arms wrapped around them so tight, bawling my eyes out. This was the moment that I knew. It had hit home. I had lost me. I was so entangled in his game of control that I couldn't see a way out anymore. It was like I had been found guilty of a murder I didn't commit, sentenced to life imprisonment and had no way of appealing. The only thing left to do was to accept that this was now my reality.

"I can't take it anymore. I don't know what more I can do to make you happy. I've fucking tried everything and it's just never enough." I sobbed it out as Aaron spat out his abuse.
"But have you tried hard enough?" he snapped back as if the past 18 months had just been a walk in the park.
"I literally have no idea what more I can do. I give up. Please just let me go." No, he wasn't

keeping me prisoner. I was physically free to leave of my own free will. Mentally though, that was a different story altogether.
"Well, go back to your mum's then. There's no point in us being together if you're not even going to try anymore. Oh, I forgot, you can't. You haven't spoken to her in months because she was more than fucking happy to get rid of you." He seemed so delighted in the opportunity to twist what had happened.
"It was easier to keep her at a distance. You said she was too interfering."
"Yeah she was, the nosey bitch should know her place."
"She barely ever said anything to you."
"And if I treat you so bad like she says I do, why is she not here for you? Probably because she knows you'll never get anybody else. She doesn't want to be stuck with you, does she?"
"She wouldn't want me treated how you're treating me!"
"Like she is any better! She is so controlling and you can't even see it for yourself because you're so thick! If she had any sense at all she'd cut you off altogether. She's not even bothered with our baby. Some nan she's gonna be."

I lost it. LOST IT! Aaron had finally broken me. I'd always been quiet. I never showed anger to this extent, or to any extent for that matter. Past experience had taught me it was safer for me to comply than to put up a fight. I'd never been good at dealing with conflict. I'd always avoided arguing. But this, in this very moment, Aaron had pushed enough buttons so I would finally flip. And I hit him.

It was a laughable attempt, it really was. I'd never swung a punch in my life – and it was pretty obvious. But I still lashed out. His reaction? He just stood over me with the most smug look on his face, and all he did was laugh. This is exactly what he wanted. He had me right where he had been dragging me down to. I had finally stooped to a level below his. As I stood up and pushed him out of my way, he fell. I didn't push him hard, but he stumbled and fell. The look on his face made me terrified. I froze. I'm so sure my blood started coursing through my body cold at this point; I couldn't take another breath. In the moment he got back to his feet, a million thoughts ran through my mind trying to guess what he was going to do next. How was he about to react?

“Well…” Aaron paused as he moved his face to within inches of mine, “I guess now we know what kind of person you *really* are.”

These words hit me worse than any punch he could throw would have done. I’ve never been the type of person that resorts to violence. I’d always done anything but to avoid such a situation. I’d always kept quiet throughout school and college to keep myself from getting into confrontation of any kind. Defending myself, whether it be verbally or otherwise, had never been my strong point. I’d never managed to completely avoid it though.

I must have been around 12 or 13 years old when I was walking to the bus stop after school with a friend. Throughout our art lesson that same afternoon there had been another girl, Samantha, that had been asking questions about the friendship – more specifically the lack of – between myself and another girl, Amanda. Somebody had supposedly brought attention to the idea that there was supposed to be a fight between Amanda and me after school that day. Notes were passed back and forth with Samantha, and I had stated that it was the first I had heard of this – my actual worst nightmare. I spent the rest of that afternoon thinking that was the end of it. I was wrong. It was only when my friend and I were halfway to the bus stop that I heard my name being shouted. As I turned around I saw Amanda and Samantha making their way towards us.

"I thought you were going to fight me?" Amanda started as she walked around me to block my path.
"No, I said it was the first I'd heard of it when Samantha told me that's what she'd heard." I tried to walk around, only for Amanda to block my path with a side step.
"Well, I've been told you've said you want a fight, so let's fight. Now!" Amanda urged as she gripped the collar on my shirt.
"I'm not fighting you. I'm going home. I didn't say I wanted to and I don't want to." I walked forwards, loosening the grip Amanda had on my collar.
"You're only scared. Why don't you fight me?" Amanda carried on as she trailed behind me.
"I'm not scared and I'm not fighting you. I'm going home." Okay, maybe I was a little scared, but I tried not to show it.

Finally, Amanda took the hint and started to walk back in the direction she came from, with Samantha in tow. We didn't get very far before my friend grabbed my attention by telling me that Amanda was running full speed towards us. As I turned around, I saw her bolting down the path headed straight for me. My initial instinct was to run. So I did. I ran as fast as I could. I didn't stop until I reached the shopping centre and I tried to catch my breath as I made my way through to the bus stop. I couldn't even say when Amanda stopped running. I just knew that I wasn't getting myself into any kind of fight that day. Maybe I was scared, maybe it was my instincts kicking in, maybe it was the opportunity to run that I'd never had in the previous years.

Sometimes I wish I had been taught how to stay and fight. To not run away from conflict or freeze in situations that didn't allow me to run. The lack of practice in standing my ground – regardless of the consequences – probably did contribute hugely towards why I had found myself allowing Aaron to chip away at me. Why I found myself giving and giving when there was no sign of him doing the same. I was under the impression that I was doing what was necessary to keep our relationship moving and make him happy, and I was never taught that it was okay to prioritise a boundary over abuse. Yes, it is an obvious statement to make that everybody just wants to be happy in life. But boundaries are important. I had zero boundaries by this point, and he knew it, and he didn't think twice about exploiting it.

The amount of abuse he was dishing out just became too much. I couldn't take it anymore. It was a huge mistake. I felt so low and ashamed for so long – a very long time – after that. I didn't recognise myself. Who had I become? This wasn't me! I was just, broken. This was definitely one of the lowest points in my life. I never wanted to be this person. And I knew I would pay the price for this. The worst thing I could have done was show him how to make me completely unravel and lose myself. And I had. It was a huge mistake to make to give him some truth to put behind all of his previously baseless accusations and opinions of me – and that's exactly what I had just done. I had just validated all of the low blows he'd ever dealt. All of the "Who would want somebody like you's" and the "I'm doing you a favour by being with you's". In one single moment, I had proven him to be the better person. Now I felt I deserved everything coming my way.

This moment was the point that I had relinquished the very little control of myself I had left. It felt as if he owned me now. There was no corner of my mind he couldn't invade with his poison. No emotion I felt could escape his manipulation. My spirit now felt shattered beyond any repair. I desperately needed to breathe, but he was *everywhere*!

When the adrenaline had died down and the reality of my actions had sunk in, I now had an onset fear; not of him resorting to violence in retaliation, although I was scared of that too, but of how he was going to use what I had just done to tear me to pieces. I had basically handed him the gun and the bullets. Him pulling the trigger was now just a matter of time…

18.
Home sweet home

The past few months had been turbulent to say the least – since I had lashed out, I felt as if I was walking a path not knowing how long I'd be walking for. I just knew the end destination was the repercussions of what I had done.

My body had finally popped a pregnant belly. I'd hidden it quite well up until around seven months – I assumed this was because I'm a tall woman. I can put more weight on than the average woman does before it begins to show, so the pregnancy remained partially hidden for a little longer than usual before a baby bump would normally begin to appear. Our baby was growing well; all was as it should have been. If I had the hindsight to ask, I would have questioned the impact that added stress would have on pregnancy and a baby's development. I never would have guessed that carrying a child whilst going through something like I was going through could have such a huge impact on a baby's development.

On the bright side, there was one appointment Aaron did manage to attend – the 20-week anomaly scan. This scan is also known as 'the gender scan'. I knew there was no way he would miss this – he wanted to find out the gender before the birth, as did I. We were so happy to discover that we were expecting a boy. A beautiful baby boy. I had fantasies about Aaron taking our son to football on a Sunday, teaching him how to fish and how to be a gentleman. A son to help protect any siblings he may have in the future. A son that would be a good man who treated people right. Somehow, my fantasies just didn't fit the reality. Yes, I had no doubt that our son could be all of those things and more. I just knew that Aaron wasn't the man to teach him them, because he wasn't that man himself. All I felt I could do at this point was hope that having a son would make Aaron want to be that better man.

We had also sorted out our problem of finding a home for us to be our own family. If we had waited for a council house, we would have been waiting years. Aaron was desperate to get us in our own home and I was desperate not to have our son whilst living with his parents. We never could have afforded private rent off my wages alone. It just didn't cover the affordability rating that we would have needed to meet to be able to afford a house. So when Aaron's mother offered a solution of her own, it was certainly food for thought. She could offer a deposit, but we would need to find the mortgage. When we found a mortgage broker that could make this work for us, it seemed perfect. Little did I know how much this would complicate things and further tie us together.

I found it difficult to accept this help. Yes, the offer was generous, beyond generous in fact, but it just didn't sit right that it was that easy for us to get on the property ladder in our early 20s with just my income to support us doing that. No hard task of saving a deposit. No trawling the property market for years trying to find the perfect house at an affordable price. It was as if I was getting a taste of Aaron's life and how it had been with having everything handed to him on a plate. It just didn't sit right with me. Maybe my intuition was telling me it was a bad idea. Maybe I was being short-sighted in doing what was best for myself. Whatever it was, it didn't feel like the best option, just our only option.

The house itself was an exact replica of my childhood home, just a few streets away from where Mum and Peter still lived. The place I hadn't visited in months, the longest time I'd been away for since we moved in there in 1995. I was just six years old, yet I remember the first time I ever stepped foot in that house like it was yesterday. I didn't really understand what the big deal was, why Mum and Peter were so excited as they stood unlocking the front door. As we walked into the hallway, the wallpaper was very dated – some floral patterns in a spectrum of brown from the '80s. I couldn't say whether the paper had always been brown or whether it was a sign of how long it had been on the walls.

I remember the downstairs being huge. Better still, I got the big bedroom, whilst my older sister got the box room. We were so excited running around the house marvelling at how big it seemed in comparison to the house we lived in previously. I didn't grasp at the time why Peter felt so proud to be in that house, but now I got it. It was *his* house. It was the house he had worked so long and hard to provide. It was the house that would become our family home. This house, that we stood in, would be the setting of so many memories in the coming decades for the four of us. The bare, black tiled floors didn't matter. The dated décor didn't matter. The only thing that mattered in that moment was the four of us sat on the solid floor in front of the window in the living room with the warm sun of May beaming through, eating the chips smothered in salt and vinegar that we had picked up from Murdishaw Chippy on our way to the house. That moment felt like home. A warm, imperfect and all-embracing home.

That felt like a lifetime away from how I felt at the prospect of moving into what would be my new home with Aaron and our son. The house was a mess. Whoever had lived there before us was very much a fix-it-yourself kind of guy and not a great one at that. Not to mention the wasp nest in the loft that had contributed heavily to the delay in the sale going through. I pushed the sale through quicker by stating that I would deal with the wasp nest of my own accord and the estate agents we were buying from didn't need to. One trip up to the loft and three cans of wasp spray later, at eight and a half months pregnant, the wasps were all gone – plus the overflow that had managed to get into the box room via the ceiling plaster board that was sagging and not fully flush. There was so much that needed doing to that house.

We had tried to rush to get it done to create our perfect home in time for our son being born but it just wasn't possible. I felt like getting to this point of being in our own home, just the three of us, with no outside interference, nobody telling us what we needed to do and when, would be just what Aaron needed to calm down and get more comfortable. I thought it would make my life easier if he had no outside stress or pressure to provide. The only thing it did was make matters so much worse, because now – when we moved into that house, four weeks after our son was due – there were no eyes watching us. More specifically, there were no eyes watching Aaron. We were isolated, alone, and when things started to escalate further, I didn't translate this into just how vulnerable I was.

19.
Giving birth to grief

It had been so long since I'd gone through a day that wasn't difficult and exhausting from start to finish, so going 13 days overdue did me no favours. I was heavy, I was slow, I was tired. Looking back over the duration of the pregnancy, I hadn't experienced many enjoyable moments. I hadn't had any burst of energy that other women talk about. I didn't embrace my baby bump like other women do; it was just the thing that made me feel as heavy physically as I felt emotionally. I had spent a long time feeling confused and like my brain was fogged, and I craved clarity. I got upset regularly and struggled to keep my emotions in check. I was exhausted with having to make every decision, not just for myself but thinking of all the possible backlashes and consequences.

I would have loved to have enjoyed the pregnancy, my first pregnancy, a little more but I felt so shackled physically, emotionally, mentally and spiritually that I just couldn't find enjoyment in anything. It was like the entire nine months was tainted with a raincloud bursting at the seams, ready to pour out everything that had been staring me in the face for the best part of two years.

I often wondered how I hadn't gone into early labour with the amount of stress I was carrying. But, 13 days past my due date, after three days of early labour, our little boy decided now was the time for me to become a mother. Around 2am on 3rd December, I was so sure I was ready to start pushing; the pain was unlike anything I had ever experienced. After an examination, I was informed that the pain I was finding intolerable had all been to get me to 4cm dilated – I had another six to go! The sheer thought of how this would all feel at 10cm filled me with dread. But there was no backing out now – this baby was coming, and there was only one way for him to arrive. To say I was scared was an understatement. One thing I was thankful for was that Mum was in the room with us. Having her around again after barely seeing her for such a long time, and with Aaron not being a great support during labour, it was a sense of reassurance that I know I couldn't have done without during the whole birthing process.

The physical transition into this next new phase of my life was excruciating, but it was made bearable – for the most part – with the help of the doctors and midwives looking after me. As soon as I was given diamorphine to relieve some of the pain, I managed to regain my centre and became a little less delirious. At least with the physical pain outweighing the emotional hurt, I felt validated in saying out loud that I was in agony, because it was clearly evident. All of the emotional hurt of the past almost-two years could never be seen, so how could I explain it? I carried this burden of war wounds that couldn't be seen by the naked eye. To the outside world, I had nothing to hide, yet I was hiding everything. I had become so accustomed to not speaking of my own pain, not communicating without being filtered by Aaron, that I couldn't even bring myself to ask the medical professionals around me to explain the steps they were taking throughout the labour and birth; I couldn't ask for pain relief or for help when I felt I needed it.

This was it. This was the point when everything would turn around and we could finally be a happy family. My heart ached for

Aaron to step up and take more control of the situations we constantly found ourselves in – the situations *he* was putting us in. Surely now he would be so much happier being able to take a hands-on approach to fatherhood. Our little boy had been unreachable to him for nine long months; now was the time for him to finally be able to pull 50% of the load. Before now, pregnancy and preparation had been little more than watching my body grow and a blurry skeletal photograph of 4 x 3in black and white contrast. I was so sure he would find some relief in meeting our son in the flesh as I was so looking forward to doing.

During labour, all concept of time seemed to completely disintegrate, like it didn't exist. The hours rolled by one after the other without any sign of slowing down. The earth didn't stop spinning for this nothing-short-of-a-miracle being performed. All of the events of labour seemed to roll into one big blur. I remember being asked if I was comfortable with my mum being present at the birth. I remember Aaron constantly being on my phone texting whoever he felt deserved the attention more than his son entering the world. I remember the room feeling very tense. I remember having to switch positions, as pushing was taking longer than it should have. I remember 'that look' being Aaron's permanent expression throughout. I remember wanting to tell him more than anything to leave but my voice had completely abandoned me. I remember how vulnerable I felt and the weight of the responsibility of bringing our son into the world safe and sound crushing me.

Roughly 15 long, exhausting hours of labour later and the midwives had determined I needed help at the final hurdle. I didn't have a clue what a ventouse was or where they planned on putting it but I didn't question it. I was so exhausted and ready for the whole labour to be over, I did what the midwives asked and at 5:23pm on 3rd December, Isaac claimed his space in this world. He was gross. He was covered head to toe in blood and I dread to think what other liquids. He was a purple-ish colour and had a very odd cone-shaped head. Within that moment when he was placed on my chest, none of that mattered. Nothing at all mattered anymore. The whole world around me just melted into nothingness. This was it. This is what my heart was beating for. This was me. In all my life I never saw myself being a mother, a nurturer, a pillar of strength, a provider. But all of that *was* me, because all of that was what he needed me to be. My perfect little 8lb 5oz representation of everything I could ever be.

As quickly as he had been placed on my chest, he was taken away again. I saw a red light flashing on the wall accompanied by a siren echoing around the room and down the corridor. Within seconds, there, at the bottom of my bed, appeared at least seven or eight additional medical professionals. The blood was flooding out of me and making its way to the floor, forming a puddle underneath the foot of the bed. I was so dazed that I didn't know what was going on and nobody explained anything to me. I vaguely heard the word hysterectomy. They couldn't mean *me*, could they? Then, in what felt like a blink of an eye, all was calm again. The doctor had found where the bleed was coming from and managed to stop it. I looked over to the corner on my right and saw Mum stood with Isaac in her arms. She was ghostly pale and had tears streaming down her cheeks. I saw Aaron slumped in a chair, barely able to string two words together. It didn't take long for me to learn that he had passed out when he saw Isaac being born. Only to hit his head on the light that was fixed to the top of the bed I was laying on when he was making his way to his feet. One of the midwives had ushered him to sit down and recoup.

As soon as I became stable again and I had Isaac back in my arms, Mum decided that was her cue to leave. I wanted to tell her to stay with me. In this moment, I lay vulnerable and helpless in a hospital bed and I felt, fragile. I had this tiny, pure life that wholly depended on me and I felt so in over my head. I hadn't prepared very well. I had done no reading or research around how to actually be a mother and I thought the biggest decision I would have to make would be breast or bottle. I didn't know what kind of questions to ask. I didn't even know how to ask for help anymore, or whether I was allowed to. I felt so suffocated by all of this responsibility, Aaron, Isaac, the house, the job, the debt, the constant level of perfection expected of me and I had no outlet for it.

Mum walking out of the door of the delivery suite was my feeling of home becoming more and more out of reach with every step she took. It was as if I was now the baby and I needed to cry out for my mother. I felt abandoned. By her, by my home, by me. I had completely abandoned myself, especially in these past few months and I had no idea how to get back to myself. The only thing I had managed to do is increase the weight of the world I was trying to drag home with me. Now that she had left the room, my cavalry was gone, and I had no idea how to rescue myself.

After speaking with my sister over the phone, I scrolled through messages to find message after message of Aaron complaining that there was too much interference from my mum – my one source of support throughout – during the whole birth process. To the point I found that I was asked if I was comfortable with my mum being present, because Aaron's dad had called the hospital – at Aaron's request – and asked for her to be removed from the room because she was making Aaron feel uncomfortable. He was more than happy to relay his feelings to me once we were alone in the delivery suite. Message after message to a lot of his friends and my sister.

There's no point in me being here.

I can't do anything with her in the way.

She's getting too involved. I need her gone.

She might as well be the baby's dad.

Did she interfere too much with your life like she's doing here?

It's pathetic. I can't even get involved in my own baby's birth.

Eventually, Aaron was asked to leave due to the hospital policy of me going to the maternity ward alone after visiting hours. Honestly, all I felt was relief. I watched Aaron, step by step, leaving the room and saying he would be back for visiting hours tomorrow. As I watched, I didn't feel how I had when I was watching Mum leave. I felt relieved and full of dread. I knew I now had some space, but I also knew I was on borrowed time because, as he had said, he would be back tomorrow. There were just a few more tests to be done before I could go up to the maternity ward. In that time I was in that room alone with my son, waiting for those tests, something came over me. I don't know if it was the comedown off the diamorphine, the intensity of the past two years, the hormones or the safety of that room and the several inaccessible doors it took to get there, but I let go.

I hadn't cried in months and I finally found myself in a safe enough place to let it all out. I gazed at this beautiful bundle of love wrapped in blue until I couldn't see him anymore through the tears that just kept coming. I needed comfort, I needed warmth, I needed support, I needed understanding. I hadn't felt any of that in such a long time. I sat on the bed and brought my knees to my chest and sunk my chin down and I sobbed so hard. I cried so hard that I was scared of bursting the stitches I had inside and out. I didn't understand what was happening to me. I didn't understand what had happened to me over these past two years but the grief was so real it was palpable.

In those moments, when I was able to lower my walls and be completely vulnerable, alone in a secure room, I opened myself up to the love radiating from the cot at the side of my bed. It felt alien to open myself up, as I'd tried so hard to keep myself closed off for a long time. I allowed myself to feel it and take it all in. I could feel it seeping right through every part of me. It felt so pure and so delicate, yet it was the most powerful I had felt in a long time. The tears flowed down my face as I wondered what kind of life I could offer my son.

I thought back to my childhood and how even though Mum and Peter were never in the highest paid jobs of incredible importance, I still never wanted for anything. I was provided for. I knew from my childhood that abundance comes from more than just money and material things. I knew that although mine and Aaron's home was a bit up-in-the-air at the moment, we would make that house a home and it would be a home we could all be happy in. It would be our place of safety and security. I knew that he was feeling overwhelmed with the whole pressure of parenthood looming and he hadn't behaved in the best way he could have towards me but I was so sure things would calm down once Isaac was born and we were settled in our own home. Life had never felt more chaotic but I was so sure I would never let that chaos reach my son.

After a good while, I managed to calm myself down and regain some form of composure, and off we went to the maternity ward where I spent three days before I was allowed to go home. I physically had a lot of healing to do because of how traumatic the delivery had been. We hadn't packed enough clothes for me or my son, as we hadn't expected to be in hospital for so long. Mum was more than happy to drop clothes in at the hospital when she visited. Even something as miniscule as that caused problems. According to Aaron, my mum was only bringing the clothes that she had bought and not bringing the clothes that we had bought. She was trying to take over again. She was interfering too much again. Everything we'd bought for Isaac was at Mum's house. I wanted to be back at home whilst I found my feet in motherhood, so it had been planned in advance that this, combined with Mum's house being closer to our house, that I would stay there with Isaac, and Aaron would be able to visit more often, as he was staying at our house anyway. Logic was never good enough for Aaron though; it was always a case of things had to be done his way.

20.
The look on the faces of those people will never leave me

During those three days Isaac and I spent in hospital, we were visited by grandparents only. Mum and Peter, Aaron's mum and dad and my biological dad. To say that I was shocked when the latter turned up on the ward is an understatement. I had confided in Aaron that I wasn't too happy with my dad having any form of relationship with me or Isaac because of his excessive drinking. We'd had a turbulent relationship during my teen years. As far as being involved in my adult life, I had made it quite clear that I would cross that bridge when the time came – at home. Aaron completely ignored these wishes and invited my dad down to the hospital without telling me he had done so. I couldn't quite figure out why he had done this. Especially as I had said it's not what I wanted. I believed it was for me to make that decision – not Aaron. He had no place getting involved, as he didn't understand how fragile the relationship with my dad was. He hadn't even met him before that day my dad came to the hospital.

After three long days on the maternity ward, I was so happy to hear a doctor tell me she was happy to let me go home. I called Aaron to let him know we were coming home that day, and he seemed excited. He responded by telling me he would get himself ready and get to the hospital so he was there for Isaac coming home. I also called Mum to let her know, as she was the one driving us home. Her response was exactly the same. When Mum reached us, she commented on how relieved and happy I looked to be getting out of the hospital; she was right. She then asked where Aaron was. He hadn't got here yet so I texted him to let him know Mum was here and we were packed and all ready to go home.

Where are you?

Just on my way. I had to get showered and go and get my hair cut.

Could you have done that another day? My mum is here and I'm ready to go. How long will you be?

About 20 minutes. Why is she there already? You should have waited for me to get there and then called her.

I rang you nearly two hours ago. I just want to go home.

Well wait there. I'm not getting there to find you've already gone because you're on your mum's watch.

I've been stuck here for four days. I want to go home. Be as quick as you can.

You're an idiot! Don't tell me what to do.

When Aaron arrived at the ward I could see in his face he was angry. He approached the bed we were at and pulled the curtains across so we were alone. Before I could pick the bags up to go home, he started again.

"Tell your mum to go and wait downstairs in her car," he barked.
"She already has gone downstairs," I replied, as she had already mentioned something about parking.
"Why is she even here? Sticking her nose in again!" I didn't have the energy to do this right now.
"She's the one taking us home she needs to be here to do that," I said as I placed the bags on the bed.
"She didn't need to get here before me though, did she?"

"I called her after you. I didn't know you were going to take two hours to get here."
"I had to go for a haircut. It's not my fault the queue was huge."
"I've been here for four days. I just want to go home."
"From now on, you do what I say when I say it. And after our house is ready, your mum can piss off. She doesn't get to say what we do and when. I thought you had learnt this by now but apparently you're still a fucking idiot," he said to me through gritted teeth as I held back tears. I knew better than to cry when he had something to say.

I picked up our bags and placed them over one arm and picked up the car seat with Isaac inside with my other hand and opened the curtains. As I made my way across the ward, I could feel a lot of eyes burning into me. I looked around the room to see the look on the faces of the other patients and their families. I could see pity and people hurting for me. Surely my hurt wasn't that obvious? I was hardly hiding bruises and covering up scars. It was as if they could all read my mind or something that I was missing was blatantly obvious.

I replayed the conversation we had just had in my mind and couldn't figure out why I was the focus of everyone's attention. I came to the conclusion that my mum getting here when she did was a terrible idea and that he was right. So the cycle started all over again. The cycle of the action that causes the argument, the abuse that follows the argument, the blame I take and apologies I make, the changes that take place to make him happy. Action – argument – abuse – blame – apology – change. The cycle that had me stuck.

21.
Behind closed doors

When we moved in to our new home, I felt completely blindsided. For the past few weeks I had been staying at Mum's and it had been a huge relief. At least at Mum's house I had that motherly guidance from somebody who had been there before. Somebody that had experienced that transition into motherhood. Somebody that would support me and help me. I know Aaron's mum would have done the same but I was at that point in my life where I just very much needed *my* mum, and she was there. Despite the fact that we hadn't had the best relationship for a while. I needed her, she knew it, she sensed it. Maybe it was a mother's intuition but she stepped up *for me*. I felt so pressurised trying to keep Aaron and I physically together as much as possible. I was starting to feel torn between stepping into my new role of 'Mum' and keeping Aaron happy. My main focus had shifted from getting the house ready to now being a mother, which was an overwhelming transition in itself, without the added pressure of keeping him happy too.

My days now consisted of feeding, sterilising bottles, nappy changing, baby weigh-in clinics, winding, health visitor appointments and everything in between. My nights looked exactly the same, minus the visitors. The sleep deprivation was hard work, but to be honest I was glad to be alone. I hadn't been alone in such a long time and it was so good to just be able to hear myself think and be able to think for myself. Those thoughts were often jumbled and didn't make a lot of sense, as I was so tired, but I was still happy to let my thoughts run away with me. My main thought being that all of this stress and tension we were going through would just lift away and everything would be so much easier once we were in our own house and living our family life at our own pace.

The whole process of buying a house had been hard. The demands from Aaron had reached a level of unattainable. I had reached a point where I really couldn't get anything right and I was so exhausted with it. Aaron was desperate to get the house ready for us to move into before Isaac arrived but it just wasn't achievable. He was quite up front about the fact that he didn't want our son born into my mum's house and he tried everything he could to make sure that didn't happen.

"Is your mum coming to help with getting this house done? I can't do it all by myself you know!" Aaron's tone just told me – I knew exactly what was coming.
"She will be over to help when she can. It's not easy with her having my sister to take care of as well," I said, walking into the living room of our new home to see how much work still needed doing.
"She said she would help, so she should pull her finger out. My mum has put money into this house for us, so your mum should do what she can as well." He followed me into the living room gesturing at everything that needed to be done.
"She will be over to help as soon as she can. She's already made a start."
"No! She thinks she can just be the cavalry now that Isaac is born and not bother with any of the hard stuff. If she wants to have anything to do with him, she best earn her place," he said, turning his back to walk through to the kitchen.
"My mum will be his nan no matter what."
"Wrong. She will only be allowed to be his nan when she's shown how much she cares

about him. Does she really want him living in a shit hole like this? I know she doesn't care about you but she should care a bit more about him." He turned to look at me as if he was waiting for some form of answer to a question I'm not even sure he'd asked.
"I'll give her a call and see if she can come today or tomorrow." He rolled his eyes as he carried on
"No, you'll tell her she has to be pulling her weight if she wants to be in Isaac's life at all." And with that, he disappeared upstairs, slamming the door shut behind him.

The disagreements we had played out differently now. Before, I would try to at least defend myself before surrendering to him. Now I only had to get a hint of where the argument was leading to and it was enough to make me give up all hope I had of putting my point across. Aaron had become somebody I didn't recognise – so had I. There was no loving moments there anymore. He never offered comfort or safety. My days now just played out in a manner of me surviving one cascade of abuse to the next. The only way I could avoid it was by being in agreement and submissive with him. The more I resisted this, the nastier he got.

Did Aaron make me angry? Yes. Did I want to fight back? Yes. Did I want this relationship to be what it was? No. But I still carried on. Partly because I had kept on telling myself that things would improve once we were a family together and could just get on with things ourselves. But partly because I was too scared to admit to myself that it wasn't working. I was too scared to say out loud that all of the sacrifices that I had made in the past nearly-two years had all been for nothing. I didn't want everything that I had done for Aaron to have been in vain. Over time, and many, many arguments, he had worn my defences away. It was now, once again, safer for me to be compliant rather than fight my corner. It was safer for me not to be on the receiving end of his ugly, destructive words.

I know that in the grand scheme of things, words are just words, but words carry something that can act as a parasite if used in a harmful way. Words have impact. I had heard enough of "Nobody else will want to be with you" ,"You're ugly", "You're not good enough" , "We don't have sex often enough", "You're not doing enough for me", "You make me feel like a failure", "You're a bitch", "What good are you to anybody?" and so on to have an impact on me. These words, these defenceless, meaningless words had now become my inner voice. It was like a cancer eating away at my authenticity and replacing it with something so destructive so quickly that I didn't recognise myself diminishing before it was too late.

My inner voice now hated me. I was a mess. I couldn't make decisions for myself or cope with day-to-day life on top of the aftermath that those decisions would have if I got it wrong. It was as if I was walking a rope bridge that was being shaken at both ends and I had to keep my balance over a 100ft drop. There was no safety net. There used to be. Sometimes, Aaron would say and do loving things that made me feel like there was still the man I knew and loved within him. Slowly but surely that man had faded. My safety net had been taken away and I was left with this beast that I felt I had no choice but to deal with every day. Even when he wasn't around, everything I did, I did with him in mind – or his reaction in mind at least. He was in my head – him and this inner voice he had created that had me faltering at every step.

My only way out now was to jump. But there was no way I was making a leap into an abyss of 100ft. Even if I did find the courage to brave the drop, what would I be left with? My inner voice was telling me I just wasn't worth it, and I believed her.

22.
Lock it down

Within just over two weeks of us being home from hospital, Aaron and I managed to get the house in some form of order so we could live there. As soon as we were behind closed doors, things went from bad to unbearable to dangerous. The very first time I felt the need to physically run away from him, it was so dark and cold outside. Everywhere was covered in ice but I didn't care. It was getting late. He had been talking about visiting his family that day and non-stop pressed the idea all day long. I was so unwell, in no fit state to go anywhere. He just didn't care though. I've no idea why he was so adamant that I had to go with him but he was.

"I just can't face going out. Can you go without me? I'll come along next time," I pleaded as I sat feeding Isaac on the sofa.
"You'd expect me to do these things if it were your family though, wouldn't you?" he snapped back.
"I haven't spent any real time with my family in months though, have I?"
"Oh, here we go, making everything about

YOU as usual. Always what YOU want, never can do things my way can we? Poor Beck!" he said in a mimicking tone, bringing himself to his feet.
"No, I'm just saying I don't expect the same from you as you expect from me," I replied, trying my best not to sound confrontational.
"Bullshit! You're always so demanding. Everything I do has to be your way or what you want. I don't get a say in it." I could sense the anger coming through in his tone.

And then it came out of nowhere. He was so angry he was shouting and I could see him trying his best to hold back rage tears. I was so scared. The way the Moses basket bounced off the wall making me flinch in defence. I knew that crying, or not reacting in the way he wanted me to, made him livid, so I tried my best to hold back the tears. I couldn't handle his abuse right now. I was too scared to move from the spot, so I bit my lip and held myself together waiting to see what he would do next.

"Go upstairs and get you and him ready. We're going to see my family." It didn't matter that Isaac would be settling for the night soon. It didn't matter that I was feeling weak and fragile still. Seeing that moses basket hit the wall and crash to the floor was enough to make me see he was serious. I had told myself he never would have done it with Isaac laying in there, but I wasn't so convinced anymore. He was so out of control now. As I reached our bedroom, I turned and sat on our bed, with Isaac in my arms, and took a few deep breaths. Almost immediately I could hear him following up the stairs. As he turned at the top, he could see that I was sat on the bed and his rage cut through all restraint with ease.

"Did I not just say get ready to go out? We're going out! Are you thick?" He started raising his voice as he walked towards me.
"I was just taking a second and finding some clothes," I replied, not that it mattered. I stood up and carried Isaac with me as I tried to gather myself.
"You're just trying to get your own way yet again. I'm so sick of your shit." He started to inch closer to me until our faces were millimetres apart. I could feel the tears slipping down my cheeks before I had chance to try and stop them.
"I'm getting him ready now." I tried to walk past Aaron, but he blocked me from going anywhere.

"Why are you crying? You've got nothing to cry about." I crouched and covered Isaac as best as I could to try and distance myself and started to sob uncontrollably as Aaron leant over me and shouted down at me, "Do you know how pathetic you look when you cry? You look like such a dickhead crying over nothing. You don't even know how good you have it. Most men would have walked away from a mess like you by now." He backed off and walked around to the other side of the bed. He lay out a snowsuit on the bed for Isaac and walked towards the door. "I hate the person you make me be. This is not me. This is all on you. I'm going outside for a cig and you're going to be ready to go out by the time I come back inside, aren't you?" I nodded, unable to look him in the face, trying to get my breath back and stop the tears from flowing down my cheeks.

He made his way down the stairs and out of the front door. This was it. I knew I had to get out. Thinking as fast as I could, I thought I would be able to run out of the back door. After I had made my way downstairs and to the back door, I struggled so much to twist the key in the lock, as my hands were shaking uncontrollably. I managed to slide the door open and close it behind me. I ran as fast as I could to the gate at the bottom of the garden. Only, when I felt the sting of the cold on my feet did I realise I was barefoot. No shoes, no socks, nothing. I didn't care. I adjusted the blanket over Isaac to make sure he was covered and carried on. I just wanted to get the hell out of there and as far away from him as possible. I tried to yank the gate open but it was jammed. In a blind panic I reached for the bolt at the top of the gate, and that's when I discovered it… Where had this padlock come from?

I knew I didn't have much time before he would realise that I was trying to run away. I turned towards the house to go back inside, opening and closing the door behind me as quietly as I could in case Aaron was already inside. I found my phone and called my mum's house as quickly as I could, and Peter answered.

"Hello?"
"Peter, can you get here as quick as you can?" I begged him whilst trying to stay quiet.
"Okay Becks, we'll be over in a minute don't worry," he replied and hung up.

That voice, the voice of the cavalry, the voice that was like a candle burning bright in the window of a house giving me hope when I was stranded at sea. I gained perspective; it was almost like that voice had helped me to gravitate back towards where I needed to be. That feeling of safety I hadn't experienced with Aaron, ever, was where I needed to be. I deleted the call from my call list and sat on the couch putting on my socks and shoes. My feet were still icy to the touch. Aaron re-entered the house and came into the living room.

"My mum will be here any minute, hurry up," he barked at me.
"Okay," I said with my head down. At this point I was terrified.
"See, it's not hard to do what I ask, is it?"
I shook my head in response as I put my shoes on.

As he walked out of the room again to answer the knock at the front door, I hoped with everything that I had that it was my mum and not his. At that precise moment, I would have given everything for that feeling of home to make its way back to me again. I needed my safety net now more than ever. This ride that I had been on for the past two years was now going too fast; it was out of control and about to crash. I had felt things were out of control before; only this time I wasn't the only person set to be collateral damage. I had my son to think of, and I was going to do everything I needed to do to make sure he had a safety net. If there was ever a time to jump off the ride before anything was done that couldn't be undone, then it was now.

23.
An angel in uniform

Happy 23rd Birthday to me! A birthday I would never forget, ever. Yet another day and night of hell. It felt like hell had become my new normal. However, this birthday would be my last with Aaron. That night I did have a few unexpected guests. Two wonderful police officers that I had the company of for the evening and into the early hours. Two police officers that would change my life. The most ironic thing is that they were there at his invite, not mine. Aaron had called the police to report an intruder in his house. Mum was there because he had spent the whole day and evening backing me into a corner and making me scared for my life and that of our son. I had no option but to call somebody for help, again. I should really thank him. If it wasn't for his outrageous attempt at whatever it was he was trying to achieve, I never would have been sent an angel in the form of the female police officer, Jo, that attended our house that night.

As I sat on the sofa in my living room with Mum by my side, I answered Jo's questions.

To be honest, it was brutal. It was the first time in so long I had been able to sit down and focus on evaluating what we were doing, how we were behaving towards each other, and it brought to light a lot of what had been kept in the dark for one reason and one reason only: he didn't want me to put two and two together and come up with four.

"So, going by what you've told me has happened here tonight, is this the first time anything like this has ever happened between you two?" Jo asked as she sat searching my face for clues.
"No, there's been a few things happen before," I said. I couldn't even look her in the eye.
"Okay, well what I can do is take some details in what we call a CAVA log. This is like a score system of how much danger you would think you're in. This helps us put together a bigger picture of what we're dealing with and it'll help us decide the best course of action." I could feel my mind starting to shut down.
"Okay, if it will help." I could feel it. This was the point of no return. If I divulged everything today, it would be the end. Was I ready for that cord to be cut? I felt as if I was

stood at the edge of the roof on a burning building and I could either risk it all and jump, or turn back and slowly burn. "Becky, it's to help you. What we're looking at here is what we would class as domestic abuse." I looked from Jo to the male officer as he sat softly nodding.

Hold up! Wait! What? No, it couldn't be, could it? I was shell-shocked at Jo's revelation looking in from the outside. I couldn't catch my breath. On the inside, I had so many questions and thoughts racing through my mind that I could barely keep up. If I were in an abusive relationship, wouldn't I have noticed? I wasn't a victim. I wasn't being abused. He's never physically hurt me. I don't hide bruises with makeup and make excuses for scars I've had.

As I sat answering the questions for the CAVA log on the reality of my situation, because, let's face it, this wasn't a relationship or love. He didn't care for me. This was now just a situation I had got myself into that had just been spiralling out of control for too long. My situation started to sink in. In hindsight, I had done a lot and given up so much to try and make us work. A lot more than some people would have done.

Yet it was never enough for him. Nothing that anybody ever did for him was enough. There I was pouring my mind, heart, soul, life, effort and finances into him and it was all in vein. I had lost my friends, family, university, money and my future. I had lost the future I could have built for Isaac.

The most painful part was that I had lost myself. Two years I had been jumping through hoops to prove that I wanted to be with Aaron. To *prove*! Why did I ever have to prove anything? I still didn't understand why I had to prove that I wanted to be in this relationship, with Aaron. I was exhausted. I can't even begin to try and explain how exhausted I was. I loved him. He said he loved me and he spent two years diminishing every piece of me he could. How could anybody hate someone, that they claim to love so much, enough to deplete them into nothing? That's exactly how I felt – I felt like nothing.

I could understand my family and friends warning me that he was no good for me, but I could also justify – in my mind – the way his behaviour may have come across in that way to anybody on the outside looking in. It was on another level though, to have a complete stranger, sat in my house, telling me that she saw things differently. That my truth, my reality was in fact just smoke and mirrors deflecting away from this lie he had created to excuse his abusive behaviour. A professional that deals with people like him and people like me on a daily basis. It felt like somebody had come along and set fire to the lies and abuse he was holding me captive in. All I could do was stand and watch as it all burned down into nothing. Before, I thought that I had given up so much of myself and my life for a healthy, loving relationship with Aaron. I was wrong. I had given up so much just for it all to become this pile of ash beneath my feet.

24.
Burning bridges

I spent the first few weeks following that visit from the police dealing with the backlash of telling them what Aaron was doing and how he was behaving. I tried to tell him so many times in so many different ways why we couldn't be together, trying to make him accept that it was over. That was a huge mistake. The more I explained myself, the more he wore down my reasons for wanting to be alone and away from him.

I opened up about how his behaviour was making me feel. I felt suffocated, stifled. I was genuinely scared of him. During the first few days of me constantly having to explain this, Aaron did what he had done for the past two years – he blamed me. He wouldn't have to do X if I didn't Y and so on. He would turn up at the house and try to intimidate me. He would keep a constant line of contact whether it be through social media or text messages. It was a barrage of abuse and deflection. The only way he ever left the house was if I called the police to help. He was arrested a few times and given bail conditions of not contacting me or coming to the house. It didn't stop him. We were now looking at criminal charges.

Aaron changed over those few weeks. His aggression dropped, seemingly, overnight. He became soft and remorseful. He started to explain how he could see what he had done wrong and how he was going to change. How he wanted to be a better man and all he needed to do that was for me to give him another chance. He was opening up to show me the man I had wanted to see for the past two years. The man I was sure was in there somewhere. I didn't want to walk away when I was so close to having everything fall into place and us being happy as a family.

Valentine's Day came around and I was struggling. I was struggling to be a single parent. I was struggling to follow the advice that the police had given me – to call them every time he turned up at the house or initiated contact. I was struggling to keep my boundaries up when he was convincing me he had changed and he wanted to be better and make us work. I felt so torn. I felt so angry with him for not changing sooner. I felt angry with myself for leaving him and I felt angry with myself for wanting to stay. I didn't feel strong enough to not need him. I didn't feel strong enough to stop loving him. I had resolved in my mind to hear him out. So Aaron came to the house on Valentine's Day to see if we could talk things through. I was adamant in my mind that if he didn't say what I needed to hear then, there was no going back.

"Thanks for letting me come over," Aaron said as I let him walk through the front door.
"It doesn't mean anything is happening. I'm just willing to hear you out – that's all," I replied as I closed the door and followed him through to the living room.
"I'm just glad you're talking to me again. These past few weeks have been hell. I just wanted to be able to talk to you – that's all." He looked me in the eyes as I sat on the opposite end of the sofa to him.
"I can't explain how you hurt me, because it wasn't just one thing. It was all these little things that had built up over time. And now to be scared of you. To have police involved. This isn't what I wanted for us or our son." I glanced over at our baby boy fast asleep in his moses basket.
"It wasn't all me though, was it, Beck? I was so stressed and scared. I didn't know how to

be a dad. You know my dad wasn't the best to me growing up, so I don't know how to be a good dad because I never grew up with one. All I need is a chance to try. I've even got myself a job and I'm trying to turn this around." His voice started breaking as he held back tears. I sat in silence as I reeled from the news that he had a job. Did this mean he was genuinely serious about changing?

"How do I know you won't treat me like shit again? I can't cope with going through all that again." I finally managed to come to my senses.

"Because this time apart has helped me see what I've done to you. I don't want to be that man that hurts you. I want us to be a family, me and you and our boy, a proper family. I want us to get married and grow old together and raise our boy together. I want you, Beck. I want you to be my wife." I could feel my brain shutting down at what he was saying.

"We've got a long way to go before any of that. We're so young and still trying to learn how to handle life. I need time. I need to see that you aren't going to be how you were before. We should start by taking things slowly," is all I could manage to respond with. But I could feel myself melting and I really didn't want to. Everything I'd needed

to hear and see him do was happening right in front of my eyes. He shuffled along the sofa until he was next to me and took my hand in his.
"I know this is hard for us. But I'm doing everything I can. I've got a job now and I see now what I've done to you and how I can fix it, but now I'm offering to fix it, you don't want what you've claimed to have wanted for the past two years? I won't wait around forever, Beck." He wasn't angry. He wasn't scaring me. Maybe he had changed. I took a deep breath and jumped in to everything I had wanted for the past two years. This was it. It was all finally coming together.
"Okay," I replied.
"Okay?"
"Okay yes, let's do it! Let's be a family and settle down and enjoy ourselves. These past two years have been hard enough. I think it's about time we were happy."
"Wow," he said as a smile he couldn't contain spread across his face. "This is amazing. This is all really happening!" He threw his arms around me and kissed me on the forehead. I flinched and nervous-excited-laughed along with him.
"Yeah, it is," I manage with my voice muffled in his chest.

Everything I had wanted had just been offered to me on a plate. And I took it. I felt relief that it hadn't ended in the police being called and Aaron being escorted away from the house – like usual. That was another thought altogether though. What would happen to the police proceedings? Well, as it turns out it was a simple process to drop the charges. The charges that were brought to Aaron were a case of me versus him and not the Crown Prosecution Service prosecuting him directly. This meant that as soon as I dropped the charges, no further action would be taken by the CPS. This was a relief. The decision was still in our hands; it made getting back on track less complicated.

I put everything into making us work after Valentine's Day. Not that I wasn't before – it just felt like we were making progress this time. I had running the house in a good routine now; it was a huge stress alleviated. It wasn't all decorated and perfect, but it was more of a home. I built a daily routine around Aaron's shifts so we could eat together and spend time together. He tried to be a more hands-on dad with Isaac. We even managed to go on a few dates. Not everything was perfect, but it was better. I just couldn't feel settled.

I constantly found myself anticipating Aaron's rage. I felt like I was living on eggshells. I wasn't doing the housework and making so much effort because I wanted to – I was doing it in a bid to avoid another one of his episodes. Aaron hadn't calmed down at all; he just found new excuses for his anger. He wasn't happy with visitors coming when he was at work. He wasn't happy with the job he had, which he blamed me for. He would tell me I'd put too much pressure on him too soon.

Having seen that the grass was not greener on the other side, I still felt obligated to stay. I had dropped the police charges and let him back into the home. We were now engaged, so how could I ever walk away now and tell people the truth without sounding like the boy who cried wolf?

25.
A yes that was originally a no is NOT consent

I was now trapped in Aaron's world with no way out. In a combined effort, we had cut off every avenue I could have taken to walk away. As the days went on, things progressively surpassed how bad they were before the police ever got involved. In the short space of two months, we were back to business as usual. This included the sex.

After the way Isaac was born and the effects that the birth process had, both physically and mentally, sex was the last thing on my mind. But it was one of the first things on Aaron's. Aaron had accused me of cheating on him with other men – in his head he had justified this as the reason why I wanted to end our relationship. It couldn't be further from the truth. I wanted nothing more than to be alone. Aaron's accusations were combined with him demanding the passwords to my social media accounts and emails – he had them before we broke up but I changed them. He also checked my phone multiple times a day – something else that he did before we broke up, too.

Sex is something I had always struggled with. Aaron knew this and he also knew why. It never once stopped him demanding it or undermining my lack of consent in one way or another. He made no effort to restrain himself from doing this again when we were trying to make our relationship work. It would be the first time I'd had sex after our son was born, so not only did I have my old vulnerabilities to deal with, but, I also had no idea whether I was healed enough physically to do it.

The first and only time Aaron and I would have sex after our son was born was enough to tell me that my body was no longer safe with him. It had only been around a week since we got back together on Valentine's Day. Aaron approached the subject of us having sex again and everything about that night would scar me for life.

"So, now that we're engaged, we should be having more sex than we did before," Aaron said as he lay in bed next to me.
"I don't know whether I can yet. I'm scared in case it hurts," I replied as I swallowed the huge lump forming in my throat.
"It's been a while now. Stitches don't take that long to heal. The midwives even said we

should do it before your six-week check and that was ages ago," Aaron replied as he interlocked our fingers and rested our hands over his stomach.
"I know, but we couldn't have done it sooner. I just don't think I'm ready yet. I'm not even on the pill again either." I could feel my entire body starting to freeze up.
"Well, that was your fault for getting police involved for no reason. We don't need contraception. We can go to the pharmacy tomorrow and get the morning after pill." Aaron moved onto his side and was now kissing my face urging my hand towards his penis. "Come on, you've kept me waiting long enough. It'll all be fine. You're probably healed by now." And with that, he climbed on top of me.

My body froze completely. I had the urge to push him off me but my arms felt too heavy; I couldn't make them move. In a matter of moments, Aaron had taken my pants and knickers off. He gripped around my knees, pulling them apart. He started to push himself inside of me. It hurt like I thought it would. Whether it was the birth, the stitches, the lack of preparation, the tensing, I don't know, but it hurt. I turned my head to the right. I couldn't look at him. I couldn't look at our son laying in his cot asleep to my left. So I turned my head, closed my eyes, forcing the tears welling up to stream down my face and I hoped it would just end quickly. It felt like a lifetime before he climbed off me and lay back down where he was.

"You do know I can tell somebody else has been there, don't you? It doesn't feel the same as it did before. You're a dirty slag." And with that he got up and went downstairs.

The next morning I woke to feed Isaac around 6ish – like clockwork. Coming downstairs had woken Aaron up and he lay on the couch watching me feed the baby. It took him a while to wake himself up and move himself to sit up on the spot where he lay.

"I'm in work at ten. What are you doing today?" He asked.
"I'm gonna pop to the pharmacy and get the morning after pill. I'll probably take the baby for a walk later on," I replied, trying not to break down at the thought of the previous night.
"Do you have money for it?" Something I hadn't even thought of.
"Yeah I should have." I picked my phone up

to check my account. Empty. “Oh, my account’s empty. It wasn’t yesterday?” My thoughts verbalised before I could stop them. “Looks like you won’t be going out today then.” I knew better than to even ask, let alone answer back.

Pending transactions showed me that my money had gone to a gambling site that day. He had stayed up gambling all night again. I didn’t understand. He had self-excluded when we got back together, just weeks before. How was this even possible?

“Oh yeah, I forgot to tell you. I couldn’t make another account in my name, so I’ve used yours,” he added as if he could hear what I was thinking.

How. Have. I. Fallen. For. This. Again. What mess was I in now? What do I even do? He knew I knew better than to ask questions. That was why he did it. He knew he could get away with it now. Not even the police could keep us apart. I was trapped. I wasn’t safe. Whether it was my body or my bank account, I wasn’t safe.

26.
Take a chance

A lot had changed in the past two years. Natalie was now a mother, too. Her beautiful baby girl was born around the time I found out I was pregnant. She made motherhood look so easy. It was as if the role was made just for her. I hadn't seen Natalie since her daughter was just a few days old. I planned on taking Isaac over there for her baby girl's first birthday. How had a whole year flown by without me seeing them again? How had it only been a year when so much had happened since?

The morning I had planned to go over, Aaron had been gambling all night the night before – something that was fast becoming a regular occurrence. The last working day had been my pay day. He would stay up until past midnight on the last working day of each month so he could use my bank account to gamble. It was as if he had completely lost control over what he was doing, like he couldn't help himself. I woke up on the morning of the 1st to discover my bank account empty, again. How much more of this could I take? I was already in arrears with the mortgage that wasn't even six months old; the rest of the household bills were a mess too.

Something in me had flipped. I confronted Aaron about what he had done. I knew better than to confront him about anything – or even ask questions – but I'd been complicit for too long.

"Where has all the money gone out of my bank?" I asked as I entered the living room, with Isaac in my arms.
"You know where it's gone. Don't ask stupid questions," Aaron said as he turned away from the computer and rose to his feet.
"When are you gonna stop? What's gonna happen when there's no house anymore? When we can't feed our son? You already have a job. You don't need to be gambling to earn money." I started to raise my voice. I couldn't help but get upset thinking about how this would end.
"I don't need this shit from you. Don't you think I feel bad enough? I don't need you making me feel any worse," he said as he walked towards where I was stood, stopping, just inches away.
"And do you think I need this from you? To

worry about paying bills from one month to the next. I'd be so much better off not having to deal with this every single month." I took a few steps back and put our son on his playmat. A part of me didn't care what the consequences for talking back to Aaron were going to be anymore. He squared up to me making sure his nose was touching my face. "Fucking go then. Nobody is stopping you," he spat through gritted teeth.
"This is my home. You should go." And just as quickly as I finished what I was saying, his hand swiped up and hit me around the back of my ear.

As I stood in shock at what had happened, he took a step back. Holding my gaze for what felt like a lifetime, I searched for horror on his face, or remorse, or shame or anything that would indicate he had acknowledged the line he had just crossed. There was nothing. I moved my gaze towards the floor where Isaac was laying and moved myself to sit down with him. Aaron made his way upstairs to get ready for work. I had a million thoughts running through my mind and they all ended at the same point – GET OUT!

As my mind raced to figure out how I could get out this time, I picked up my phone and texted Natalie as fast as I could.

Hey hun, so sorry I can't make it today. Something has come up and I need to sort it out. Any chance you could tell Aaron I did come to you if he asks? X x

Hi Becks, don't worry it's fine. You know I will. Hope everything is OK, love you x x

I deleted the texts quickly after, so all I had to do was go to Mum's as soon as Aaron left for work. I planned on packing a few things and getting us to safety. I missed safety. I can't remember the last time I didn't spend the whole day on high alert. As I dialled Aaron's mum's number to ask her to take him to work, my mind trailed back to a conversation I'd had with his dad just a week before.

I had found receipts for a pawn brokers. The description was '9ct gold bracelet' and '9ct gold necklace'. I knew they weren't mine. I'd always worn silver or white gold, never been a fan of yellow gold. The receipts I'd found were dated just a few days before I'd found them. I knew his mum wore a lot of gold jewellery so I asked her if she was missing any. Later, I received a call back from his dad asking me to hand over the receipts. His exact words – *We won't tell Aaron that you told us about this because we don't want you to be in any danger. Just be careful* – told me everything I needed to know about how aware his family were of what was going on.

Aaron's mum came to the house to pick him up for work and she knew that something had happened. I told her about the gambling. I told her about the argument. I told her about Aaron hitting me. She didn't have much to say about it. Almost as if she knew she shouldn't be getting herself involved. Aaron came downstairs and they left after he barked at her about being late. As soon as they left, I took Isaac upstairs, placed him in his cot and started putting our clothes in bin bags.

It wasn't long before I was disturbed by a knock on the door. My heart sank. Surely, it couldn't be Aaron trying to catch me out. I looked through the glass at the top of the door from where I was on the stairs to see Aaron's mum and dad stood on the doorstep. I let them in, as I wondered whether Aaron even knew they were here. They seemed as on edge as I felt. After a swift conversation about what had happened that morning, they handed me an envelope full of cash – it was my whole month's wage. I was taken aback. I couldn't quite figure out why they would do this. Then it dawned on me – they knew I was planning on leaving. They told me that I'd never be able to leave. The police wouldn't believe a word I said after I had already retracted one statement. The house was tied up to both of us. I was stuck. I was stuck here, with him, and that was my bribe money. If I were to ever sell my soul to the devil I'd just been quoted a price.

I slowly started to see that leaving would be a whole lot harder than just packing my bags and walking out. I was financially obligated to pay for that house for the next 35 years. We were obligated to raise a son together for the next 18 years. The thought of that filled me with a sense of desperation. If the past two years had me feeling as low as I did now, what would be left of me at the end of seeing out all of our joint obligations?

27.
You choose!

Aaron never laid a finger on me again after that day. He didn't have to. I had learnt the hard way what was the safest way for me to live. Don't answer back, don't question him, don't expect anything of him. His temper was still at the forefront of his behaviour though.

Having so many restrictions, however, I was bound to slip up sooner or later. Then it happened, an accidental slip of the tongue on my part, calling the house *my* house, had him throwing a plate of hot food across the living room, landing just inches away from our baby. Isaac began to cry out. It was all the wake-up call I needed. Not just Aaron but also his family had tried to keep me in place, but never would I let it happen at the expense of my son's wellbeing.

As soon as Aaron went outside to smoke, I locked the door behind him – locking Isaac and I in the house. I picked up my phone and called the police. The police operator stayed on the other end of the phone until officers got to my house. They saw this incident as arrest-worthy and took Aaron into custody.

Only this time they had to inform Child Protection Services, as there had been a domestic incident with a child present. I didn't quite understand the repercussions this would have; I was just so happy they were taking Aaron away – even if it was only a temporary measure.

Aaron was released from custody with the same bail conditions as before – to not contact me directly, only via a solicitor in the case of child contact and not to be present in the street where our house was. He broke his bail conditions on numerous occasions. He was turning up at the house uninvited nearly every night. I had my address put on rapid response after the first few calls to the police. He would constantly call and text. He would use friends, both his and mine, to try and initiate contact. The only thing I had to do was keep reporting it to the police, which I did.

Child Protection Services arranged to come out to meet us to see if there was any way they could support me during what can only be described as a living nightmare. The house was still not great – it was liveable, just not homely or welcoming, so they came to visit us at my mum's address. The two women from Child Protection Services went into great detail about just how much they could actually do for me. They were also very clear about what would happen if the relationship between Aaron and I would resume.

"So, it's happened a few times, the relationship breaking down and you two getting back together again?" one of the women asked me as she sat with a pen in hand, writing notes as I spoke.
"Yeah, the police have been involved before but I retracted my statement when we got back together," I said as I tried to make out what she was writing down.
"And what makes this time any different?" she asked, pen still scribbling away.
"I've had enough. It's not safe for me there, or our son." I shifted uncomfortably where I was sat on the floor.
"I'm glad you see that. I'm sorry you've had to go through this ordeal. But our main priority is supporting you in keeping little one here safe," she said, softly smiling in Isaacs's direction. "We will always work with families to keep them together. I know a lot of people panic at our involvement because there is a stigma there that we are only there to take your child away. It's 100% not the

case. We're there to ensure the safety of the child. We can see that you're happy to take the necessary steps to keep your son safe. You're working with the police and you've got a great support network here with your mum and family." I nodded as I listened to what the outcome of the meeting would be. "We're happy to refer you back to police protection only. We will become involved again if Aaron was to be living back at home with you and Isaac. We would see this as a compromise of your son's safety if he was living in a home where these things were happening again. We would then have to look at how we could best safeguard your son because you wouldn't be."

Loud. And. Clear. The only thing I'm hearing from all this is the choice has been given between Aaron and Isaac. Of course my son comes first. Trying to deal with Aaron's behaviour wasn't easy right now. I had a lot of help though, with the police on board and being able to speak to my family whenever I wanted to again. It was a lot easier. It was wearing me down, but at least I wasn't living with it.

The woman from Child Protection Services was right. I was scared that she was there to take my son away from me. My very reason for being at the moment – my only reason – he was my strength throughout this whole mess. On the days when I felt like I couldn't take any more or that it would have been easier to give Aaron what he wanted when he was demanding, I'd think of the kind of life that was providing for Isaac. I knew I wouldn't be able to live with myself if anything happened to our son, or if he turned out to be just like Aaron, or just like me putting up with another Aaron. He deserved more. He deserved a real chance at being given a good, stable life. Aaron clearly wasn't about to change any time soon, so it was up to me to provide that for him. I made a promise the night that he was born, just me and him in the hospital alone, and I intended on keeping it.

If calling the police constantly and being harassed, stalked, talked about, mithered and intimidated were barriers I had to overcome to give my son everything he deserved, then overcoming them was a small price to pay.

28.
I had become a sitting duck

Aaron was arrested on a number of occasions – I lost count when it started to become a daily occurrence. He would start out with texting me. The lack of response on my part would prompt him to call. I'd turn my phone off and unplug the landline once those calls became back-to-back, relentless invasions of headspace. Once he had no way of contacting me directly, he would turn up at the house that had failed to become the answer to all of our problems. As days went by and he grew more and more desperate to get to me, he started to become dangerous.

He took any and every opportunity he had to get into the house before I had chance to call the police. He was always too late, as I had started calling as soon as I knew for sure he was there. I wasn't taking any chances. I was scared of this man and scared of what he was capable of. He tried to write it off as an attempt to fix our relationship – leaving flowers and gifts in the back garden. He'd broken the locks on my back door with a rock from the garden. The real eye opener of just how far he was willing to go came when he managed to climb through the smallest window of the kitchen.

I spent every day waiting for the next incident. Waiting for him to show up. Waiting for him to do whatever he was going to do that day. Bail conditions meant nothing to him – he just saw them as a reason not to get caught doing what he was doing. I was frightened of this man that had emerged so far away from the man he portrayed himself as when we first met. As time went on and Aaron became more unravelled, it was so obvious that he had *told* me the man he was; I didn't actually *see* that man though, not ever. The man he really was sprung up and wrapped his rapidly growing vines all around me until I couldn't move. It felt so suffocating and restricting. Before this, his words were enough to reel me in and anchor me down to him – below him in fact – and any time he thought I may be at risk of cutting the chains, he showed me a glimpse of the man he told me he was. A glimpse was all it had taken, every time, to wind me back in again.

As soon as Aaron started to see that the words and the glimpses didn't cut it for me anymore, his attention turned to trying to provoke a reaction from me. He spread a lot of lies about how our relationship had broken down because of things I'd said or done, because of the way I had behaved towards him. He was so desperate for people to believe his version of events that he was happy to throw me – the woman that he claimed to love and harassed and stalked with the excuse of wanting to resume the relationship – under the bus.

The realisation of how dangerous this unrecognisable man was getting hit home when, one morning, Peter returned home from work within an hour of leaving after being attacked by Aaron. Again, there was barely any proof for the police to press charges with. Aaron had become a master at his own game. I started to become doubtful that the police would ever be able to protect me from him. I didn't doubt their capabilities to do their job. I was just becoming more and more aware that there is a certain level of proof needed for the Prosecution Service to be able to convict successfully. Aaron was an expert of manipulation at this point; only it wasn't me he was manipulating anymore – it was the grey areas of the law.

That Friday that he managed to gain entry through the kitchen window into the mound of bricks and mortar that didn't feel like our home anymore landed him in police custody for a whole weekend. Finally some relief. Or so I thought. Having that breathing space for the weekend enabled me to gain some form of clarity on my life as it stood at that moment. Reflecting on the previous two years, I couldn't help but feel a huge sense of grief. For everything I was before, for everything I had lost. I needed to mourn because I had left myself so far behind in the name of this love that had just left me feeling empty. So much of myself and my life had changed that I felt like I was inside of this shell that I had no idea how to fill. My home was just an empty shell. My relationship had just turned out to be an empty shell. I had been left as a shell of a person.

My silver lining to this earth-shattering storm I was trying desperately to weather was this beautiful baby boy that I had been gifted. This tiny human that was relying entirely on me to provide and protect. With him, I was given a sense of purpose. A purpose so overwhelming that I had learnt very rapidly that I was willing to do anything to fulfil that purpose. I had been given a reason to keep going and to not give up on myself. When I was doing it for myself, I had given up months before. I had accepted that Aaron and the life I had with him was my lot. Now that I had this whole new purpose, my perspective had completely changed. Even with all of the motivation I could ever need, I still felt incapable of fulfilling this purpose.

I spent the whole weekend trying to relax and took the time to gather myself together. At the back of my mind though, I knew the peace would only last a weekend. I knew that, come Monday morning, he would be in court to answer to breaking his bail conditions and would be let back out onto the streets. I knew Aaron was smart and could play along the line drawn by the law. I had no idea how I was going to cope with this for what I felt like was going to be the rest of my life. I felt I couldn't go out anymore because I was vulnerable, reachable, accessible. I felt like I couldn't stay home because I was a sitting duck just waiting for him to turn up whenever he pleased.

My mind had now trapped me into thinking I was stuck between a rock and a hard place. I'd never be able to just have a normal life again. I'd always be linked to Aaron; we had a child together – of course I would always be linked to him. I would always have to deal with constantly keeping him at arm's length and not letting him reel me back in.

I thought a lot about the words Aaron said to me when we first met, *"Are you ready for the first night of the rest of our lives?"* Those words that once gave me butterflies and made me lightheaded now filled me with a sense of dread. How were the "*rest of our lives*" going to look? Would it be a game of Aaron trying to force his way into my life and me fighting him off until one of us gave up? I knew I'd never be able to hold out for years – I was exhausted with it all in a matter of weeks.

The worst part of trying to figure out what the future would look like for us was trying to figure out how we would ever be able to co-parent our son. How would we have conversations about how our son was doing, school progress, arranging holidays and special occasions if the only contact we were supposed to have was via a solicitor? Would our son have a healthy outlook on life and relationships with us being the example set for him? The hardest part of all of the questions I was facing around co-parenting was, how would we ever deal with a second child being thrown into the mix if we were failing already with the first?

29.
Sometimes the thing that needs doing isn't what you want

I thought back to that night. The night I felt his weight pushing me further and further into the bed. I thought about how I tried to hold my tears back for fear of how Aaron would react if I had let them flow. The night I couldn't bring myself to look left, because how could I ever set eyes on a pure, innocent life that relied on me for protection when, in that moment, I failed to protect myself on so many levels? It was because of my failure to protect myself that I was now paying the price.

I thought back to when I found out that I was pregnant with Isaac. I thought about how happy I was because I genuinely believed that a child was the answer to our problems – the answer to me being at the base of Aaron's problems. I didn't feel the same this time. I knew this time it wouldn't be the case. The man I thought Aaron was turned out to be some fictional character. In reality, what I was dealing with was an abuser.

I thought about how Aaron was shaping up to be a dad for our son. Although I knew I was the one creating that barrier for the sake of my own safety and sanity, I was also so upset at how Aaron wasn't treating our son as a priority. His fixation was on *me* and keeping *me* where he wanted to be so he could make his own life a lot easier.

I thought about how I would cope with two children so close in age, on my own. I was a single mum. I had to face the reality of that. One thing I was surprised about was even though I was waking through the night, dealing with teething and trying to find the perfect nursery for Isaac now that my time was coming around to be back in work, it was still a lot easier than being under the weight of Aaron's expectations.

I thought about our son. He had already been through so much in his short life. He had already had one parent decide he wasn't a priority. He deserved my attention. He deserved my time and commitment. He deserved a proper, focused mum. This baby also deserved so much more than I felt capable of giving. I was still in such a fragile state that I was struggling with just him. Could I really cope with two? I knew the answer. I knew in my heart what the best thing to do was. It just wasn't easy.

At one point I felt like my support network was nowhere to be seen. My safety net had disappeared and I was just falling into an abyss. I fell a pretty long way down before I bounced off the intertwined fibres that made sure I didn't hit rock bottom. My safety net was there, and it was a lot bigger than I could have ever expected. I knew my nan coming with me to the doctor's office would forever be proof that a little faith, no matter how scary the fall, would always see that rock bottom was never reached.

"So, what can I help you with today, Rebecca?" the doctor asked as I sat awkwardly in the solid chair next to her desk.
"I'm pregnant," I managed to blurt out before trying to say the next part without using the A word, "but I need not to be."
"Okay. May I ask, have you taken a test?" she replied and I gave a look that I'm sure she picked up on. "It's procedure that we have to ask that you're sure you're pregnant before we take this any further."
"I have. I'm sure." I looked down, partly in shame, partly in embarrassment that I was even having this discussion.

"Okay. May I ask your reason for not wanting to be pregnant anymore?" I was shocked at the lack of judgement coming from the doctor. I looked at my nan, searching for reassurance. It was as if she knew exactly what I needed in that moment. She gave a nod and half-smiled, holding my hand as I went on to explain.
"I already have a son. I'm not with his dad anymore though who is the father of this child, too." I took a breath. Was this the moment I say I felt forced? It's not enough to *feel* forced though, is it? You actually have to *be* forced. So what's the point in saying it if I actually didn't technically say no? So I stayed quiet and continued, "We're not together anymore. It's quite messy and the police are involved. I just feel it wouldn't be fair to bring another child into the middle of it all." The doctor nodded lightly and continued on with explaining how the referral process for abortion works.

I left the GP feeling numb. I knew I was making the right choice for the right reasons. Though I still felt terrible. *Some mother I was shaping up to be* is the only conclusion I kept on coming to. It was only a matter of days after that appointment before I was in the abortion clinic, Mum by my side. I got sent the details of the clinic, no hospital or GP practice. It was just a regular house on a regular street of Liverpool.

Liverpool. I had missed it so much. The last time I was here was when I was still going to university. I missed uni, too. I missed who I was then. At that time that I was becoming everything I ever could be and more. It was a far cry from the reason I was in Liverpool on that day, for that reason. I felt so far away from myself – like I was thinking of two entirely separate people. I had let go of myself so easily for the sake of somebody that did nothing but use me for two years. Aaron had used my mind, my heart, my body, my bank account for two whole years and I believed that it was love. Going to Liverpool that day was so painful for me on so many levels.

After we were done at the clinic, I stayed at Mum's house for a few days to physically recover and to prepare myself for the trial that was set for just three days after. The weight of my reality was eased so much because, well, I was home. I was back in those four walls that had been home for the previous 15 years. I felt safe, for the first time in a long time. I could let my heart beat without fear of it beating too loud.

My home, the place that I had needed to be at, to visit, to return to for so long had finally managed to call me all the way back to it. If only for temporary relief, it was better than feeling stranded in the middle of a life that felt like quicksand. The home that had seen me through my earliest memories of my childhood, my yellow and blue themed bedroom with the blue painted floorboards and the bunk beds that I didn't need because I was the only person who slept in that room. The endless hours of fun with my older sister, sliding down the stairs on our mattresses and me staying up past the hours I should have to watch her play Resident Evil and Tomb Raider on her PlayStation. The house of safety that saw me through the transition into high school, which I didn't cope very well with. The endless amounts of sleepovers I had with my childhood best friend. I would watch Mum plough through hours of ironing, whisper-singing Robson & Jerome on her huge stereo with big headphones that were pointless because she played her music so loud we could hear it anyway. The meticulously decorated walls and matching colour schemes for the furniture that Mum would put so much effort into year after year. The place I discovered I didn't want to be a hairdresser and that I was more suited to studying business. The house I came home to and cried in Mum's arms because I'd passed my driving test on the fifth attempt. The home I loved so much that I commuted an hour each way to attend uni because I didn't want to leave. The home that saw me stepping into adult life with my first job. If the walls of that house could talk, they would have so much to say.

All I needed, on that day, was for those walls to stand. To stand and shelter me like they had done for so many years through so many memories. For those four walls to close their entries and keep me and my son safely tucked away inside. It was only for a few days, but those few days were all I needed from those walls of that home.

30.
I will find my voice

To say that I was feeling fragile would be an understatement. As I stood outside the court room in the waiting area with Peter and Natalie, I was greeted by the prosecution barrister.

"Hi, is it Rebecca?" She looked between Natalie and me to see who would step up.
"Yes, that's me," I said, raising my hand a little.
"Hi Rebecca, how are you feeling today?" she asked, extending her hand.
"I'm tired but okay. I just want all this over with," I replied nervously as I shook her hand.
"Well, that's understandable. Now I know you've had a medical appointment in the past few days that may excuse you from giving evidence in court if you're not feeling 100% up to do so?" I wondered whether she could see how I really felt as I stood shaking on the spot.
"I can give evidence, I think." I had a huge ball of anticipation taking over in my stomach.

"Okay, I will let the judge know anyway just in case you do need to be excused. So what happens today is I will be putting the charges and evidence before the judge and the defendant then gets to put his plea forward. If he pleads guilty then you won't have to give evidence. The judge will listen to the defence and will decide an appropriate punishment from there. If he pleads not guilty, it will go to trial and evidence will be heard from all sides. The judge will then make a decision based on all evidence presented. Have you got any questions or anything you would like me to know beforehand?" she asked as I tried to digest everything she had just said.
"No, not that I can think of," I replied, and Peter quickly followed up with his own question.
"Would you be able to tell us if it's a public gallery?" Peter asked, grabbing the attention of the barrister – I was grateful he'd asked.
"Yes, it will be, so you'd be more than welcome to sit inside and hear the hearings and the trial." Peter nodded in an approving way. "Okay, so I'm just going to catch up with the judge now and find out when we're due to go into the hearing." With that, the prosecution walked away.

A short while after, everybody was inside the court room – Peter and Natalie included – and I sat waiting on the outside in the corridor. The prospect of having to give evidence in a courtroom, in front of a judge, started to dawn on me. How could I ever try to explain to a judge, in front of a defence – somebody who has spent their whole career picking holes in evidence – what had happened to me. *I* didn't fully understand what had happened to me. All of my memories were jumbled up and I couldn't pinpoint exactly what had happened and when. I couldn't find the words to explain his behaviour because I was still confused as to when his behaviour that he described as love had turned into something that wasn't love anymore. And if it wasn't love, then what was it? I didn't know. I couldn't take the stand and give evidence of something I didn't know.

The only thing I did know was that I felt like a fool. I felt like I had been in an entire relationship with nobody. I felt like I had bought a house with nobody. I felt like I had a baby with nobody. The man I thought I knew was nowhere to be seen and hadn't been for a very long time by this point. In his place stood a stranger. A stranger that I was scared of. A stranger that had tricked me, robbed me, conned me, taken me for a fool, abused me, used me. I felt like some sort of overdramatic imposter giving intimate and detailed evidence on the behaviour of a complete stranger. Yet this complete stranger was inside my head. He could tell you what was written all over my heart. He knew how to control my mind. He knew how to manipulate me. How was any of this fair? I had given so honestly to a man that had done nothing but lie.

The door to the courtroom swung open disturbing my train of thought and out came the prosecution, swiftly followed by Natalie and Peter. As she approached me, I stood up from the fold-down chair where I was sat.

"Okay, so he has pleaded not guilty, so it will be going to trial. Do you still feel capable of giving evidence?" she asked as I tried to figure out how my lungs worked.
"Yeah. I mean I don't want to but I will."
She gave a nod of sympathy my way,
"Right, well I will just go and confer with the judge and see what will happen going forward."

The prosecution was only gone a short time before returning to me - with a trump card.

"So, I've spoken with the judge and defence. Because of the amount of evidence there that suggests the relationship was very on-off, there is a good chance he will be found not guilty if he insists this was the case whilst the police were in attendance." I tried to gather my thoughts. All of the agony of the past few months, for what? The prosecution continued, "There is also the matter of the fact that you're not in denial that the baby you were recently carrying was his…" she paused to gauge what my reaction would be.
"The baby was his. I wouldn't lie about something like that," I responded, knowing exactly what he was going to do with this information. Obviously there had to be sexual intercourse for conception to take place. I just wasn't ready to open *that* can of worms.
"In that case, the judge has stated that he is willing to grant a non-molestation order to keep the defendant away from yourself if we can skip the trial. How would you feel about that?" she asked, scanning my face, waiting for me to say something.
"What's a non-molestation order?" I felt stupid for asking the question but needs must.

"It's basically like a restraining order. It will state he can't be within a certain distance of you and can't contact you directly. It has a lot of clout in court, too, if he chooses to ignore the order," she explained as I'm sure she spotted the lightbulb illuminate above my head.
"I'd be so happy with a restraining order. I just want to be left alone." A tear ran down my face as I realised how tired I was. Physically, mentally, emotionally, I was just so tired.
"Okay, I'll let the judge know you're happy with that and get that sorted." She touched my arm in compassion and walked back towards the court room.

I was left wondering whether I had sold out. Should I have gone to trial and tried to get a harsher punishment? I guess with evidence such as a baby it's pretty easy to paint the picture of me being the 'psycho girlfriend' who would lure him over and call the police in an attempt to whatever he tried to imply I was doing. A small part of me had wondered if that day in court was going to be *my day*, my Erin Brockovich moment. The moment I exposed everything and left no shadow of a doubt in anybody's mind that this man was abusive. It would have been nice, but as quickly as I thought it, I'd resigned myself to the fact that I wasn't strong enough to do that.

I had spent the last two years in a game I wasn't even aware was being played. I'd finally figured out how to quit, so I just wanted out. No sooner had the dust of the day settled when Aaron decided that he wasn't ready to let me quit without finishing his mission.

The following day, I was at the house with Isaac, and the lack of pings-on-phones and knocks-on-doors was eery, too eery in fact. It didn't take long for the landline to start its usual tune.

"Hello?" I answered, feeling upbeat that Mum was probably calling to check up on me.
"Hiya, it's only me." This had to be a joke? Why would Aaron's dad be calling after yesterday? I was in stunned silence as I gripped the receiver tightly. "I just wanted to say thanks for yesterday. I mean for agreeing to a restraining order and not having Aaron punished any harsher than that." The line went quiet.
"I just want to be left alone," was all I could

manage before I put the handset back down on the base.

Within seconds, the landline started to ring out again. I had a sinking feeling this was far from over.

"Hello?" I said, quite abruptly.
"Thanks for doing that yesterday, Beck."
My blood ran cold and I slowly put the handset back on the base again without saying a word.

Of course Aaron would call. He hadn't been playing by the rules since day one. Why would a piece of paper change his mind now? That overwhelming feeling of suffocation came over me again as I started to panic. It was quite clear that the end wasn't actually going to be the end. It was just the beginning of the end.

I still craved my voice. I still craved to speak my truth. Maybe court the previous day wasn't the time or place for me to do that. But I knew that no matter what my voice may sound like, whatever words I would use, however long I would have to wait and however loudly it came out, I would speak *my* truth. Whenever that day may be, I would speak the whole truth, because I had nothing to hide.

Epilogue

The police took no further action after Aaron had made contact with me less than 24 hours after being granted a restraining order – lack of evidence. They also took no action over the attempts he made to contact me via other people. The only contact I was able to receive from him was via a solicitor in regard to the matter of his contact with Isaac. In respect of the court order, I feel it wasn't worth the paper it was written on as Aaron was still finding those grey areas within the law to continue his abuse. The only thing it really gave me was space, just not enough of it. It wasn't the clean break I hoped it would be when I walked away from court that day.

I made sure I appointed a solicitor straight away. It took Aaron 9 months to bring up the matter of contact with Isaac. My solicitor was really good in the respect of filtering what they forwarded to me and when. They took a lot of abuse from Aaron simply because they weren't willing to give all the contact he wanted – they were doing as I instructed. The feeling of having a team working *for me* was amazing. I finally had a team backing me up after so long of fighting against Aaron and his family and feeling alone in doing that.

The aftermath of abuse got a whole lot worse for me before it got better. I was diagnosed with depression, anxiety and post-traumatic stress disorder. It drove me to the brink of suicide. I reached out to a local charity and used a their counselling service. The house was sold and I moved to a neighbouring town with Isaac for a fresh start. I bought my own car. I severed so many ties I had to Aaron in the way of mutual friends and acquaintances.

For a long time, especially immediately after the court date, I was still scared to leave the house. I was scared to speak to people and I constantly questioned whether there were people watching me and reporting back to Aaron. I constantly kept all of my doors and windows locked, even in the summertime, and even when I moved towns and Aaron didn't know where I lived. I didn't have the confidence to live outside of my own life and dream big again, until now, ten years on. Now my dream is to help other women that have experienced or are experiencing the same things I have. Nothing to Hide is my way of sharing my story to help anybody that needs to know that they are not alone.

Lightning Source UK Ltd.
Milton Keynes UK
UKHW020635180721
387330UK00002B/3